MARKETING USING AI IN DIGITAL SPACE

Dr. Pooja Kudesia

Made with ❤ on the Notion Press Platform
www.notionpress.com

Dedicated to my biggest critics,

My Kids

Author Profile

Dr. Pooja Kudesia Srivastava is a passionate educator who is also the founder of the 'Formatuer', a blended learning platform for advanced digital marketing skills. She is also an avid follower of startups and hackathons and have been recognized by the Ministry of Education and Information Technology for featuring in top 300 ideas at 'Hack theCrisis', 2020. She is on the book review and module development panel of Tata Mc Graw Hill, Oxford Publications and MIBM Global. She is also a Black Belt in Six Sigma and a key Resource Person for faculty development programs of Jagannath University, Jaipur.

Preface

Online channels have gained increasing presence in the sales funnel. The functioning of online channels has seen a sea change due to the advent of AI. This change has been primarily perplexing for marketing and sales professional as many fail to grasp the difference between AI, ML and Deep Learning. In fact, AI has become omnipresent in all domains of online marketing including search engine optimization (SEO), content strategy, customer analytics and creatives.

This book has been written for professionals and aspiring executives in the field of marketing and sales. However, it is equally interesting for professionals of other domains also. For example, in the case DaVita: A kidney care company faced the challenge of hiring the right medical practitioners in an intensive competitive labour markets and tighter budgets. While social media is typically the domain of marketing, and recruitment usually belongs to HR. DaVita's teams collaborated and were successful in driving 42% more job applications.

The book aims to provide a glimpse of AI in marketing as well as serve as a study guide to navigate the field. It also showcases brands across the globe who have put Google's generative AI to work.

Reach out to me with your feedback at https://x.com/formatuer_in

Contents

Contents

Exposition:
Part I

Marketing in the Digital Space

The world has changed dramatically after the launch of Web 2.0. This new version of internet has not only enabled consumers to be content creators but has also empowered marketers to be not only thrift in the marketing expenses but also derive a higher ROI on their expenses as compared to offline marketing avenues. As per hubspot, there are 2.71 billion shoppers who are present online and prefer to avail the benefits of online shopping[14]. This dramatic shift in the consumer's behavior has warranted the marketers to have meaningful online presence. This might be through websites, email, blogs or social media. It has given birth to the online marketing also known as digital marketing. Digital Marketing helps brands and companies to customize their communication to the customer so as to move up the brand pyramid. Digital Marketing has enabled this communication to be not restricted to text. It has taken the form of video, text and audio i.e. podcast.

Digital communication has enabled the consumers to learn better about the brands. The consumers are able to learn about the parent company, the suppliers, brand ambassadors, employees, co-brands as well as the well as the buyer reviews. It has also enabled the marketers to gain tremendous consumer faith in their respective brands. As per research by GWI, a typical user spends 2 hours and 23 minutes per day on social media. This means that he/she is spending 35. 8% of online time on social media activities[42].

The use of digital strategies and tactics has also enabled the marketers to be at the place where consumers spend most of the time. Depending on their goals, they can support both large and small campaigns though the free and paid channels which are at their easy disposal. For example, a marketer might use blogs on the website to generate leads for their campaign. Similarly, he/she might make good use of influencer accounts on social media platforms to attract interest in the brand. These campaigns are likely to be more effective than offline marketing campaigns as they are more specifically targeted towards their prospective customers. All the more they are more cost effective in not only in terms of financial expenditure but also in terms net reach to the larger audience. The marketing of brands in the online space also enables more leads, better conversion rates at the same time increasing engagement with the audience. Let us discuss in detail:

1. **Targeted Campaigns:** When a marketer places an advertisement on a roadside hoarding (billboard), the rental value of the site is determined by the location, amount of traffic, size of the hoarding, time length for which the site is being hired.

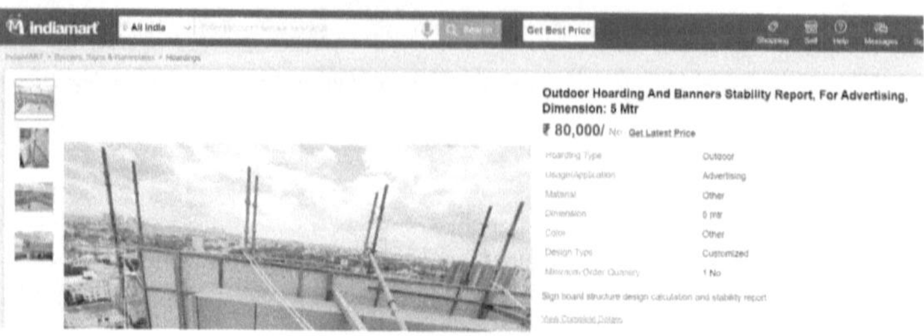

These parameters are not in favor of the marketer as he/she has no clue of the demographics passing though the site. Moreover, it renders no space for customization of messages to the audience. Thus, the investment in the roadside hoarding might raise the brand awareness, but makes little sense on the sales conversion.

2. **Huge Opportunity for small time Marketers:** Investment in online marketing is conversely much cheaper and offers better return on investment as it quite measureable. It also offers the smaller brands to compete with the larger players on a level playing field. The metrics and performance dashboard offered by Facebook gives a glimpse of this.

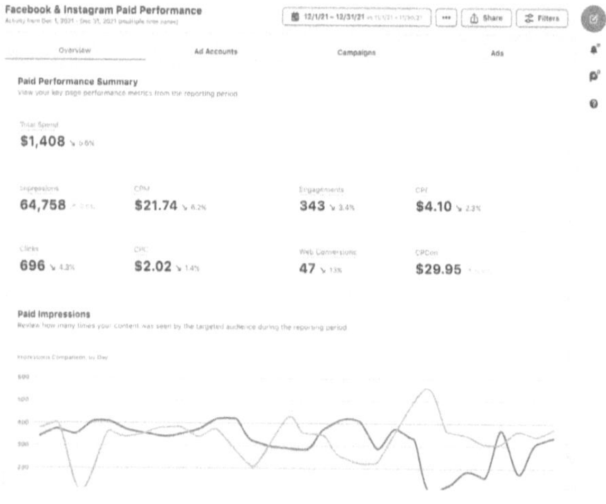

3. **Online Marketing helps brands to effectively engage with the prospect and customers:** Modern day prospects and consumers are much more informed, thanks to Web 2. 0. They are aware of competing brands, their products, features, availability and price. This very much shifts the power balance in favour of the prospects and consumers rather than the sales representatinves. Therefore in order to be successful, sales representatives need to be better informed about the buyer`s journey (Awareness→Consideration→Decision Stage)[3]. They need to provide a helping hand to the prospects at every stage rather than adopt pushy sales tactics. Let us look at the buyers journey in detail and see how online marketers can help sales representatives in closing the sales.

The buyer`s journey is nothing but a path to purchase of the brand. In most of the purchase decisions which are not impulsive, the buyer takes his/her time to become aware, consider, evaluate and thereby take the decision to purchase a product/service. This journey is fraught with painful experiences and problems which can be social, psychological or financial. However, if the sales representatives are able to understand the factors shaping the buyer`s thinking, they would be able to empathize with the buyer and position the brand better.

So how can online marketing help resolve the painful experience encountered by the buyer in his journey. Let us examine each of the phases distinctly:

Awareness Stage: At this stage, the prospective buyer becomes aware about the problem either by personal examination or by the social and economic influence. The buyer experiences the need for loads of information on the problem and its resolution. For example, a prospective buyer might have developed black heads on the face. This development on his skin might have been bought to notice by his friends / relatives / family who might have passed negative comments on this display photo. The negative comments have already created a painful rendition in the mind of the prospect. At this stage, he/she is no mood for being pursued for sale. Instead they are looking for help in the form of information regarding goals of problem resolution, challenges involved in the resolution, consequences of non-redressal and misconceptions. Providing resources containing detailed information is likely to be well received by the prospect. This is where the online marketing makes a mark in helping the sales representatives with blogs, articles, videos and podcasts which position the brand uniquely addressing the problem. This unique feature is unavailable in offline marketing.

Consideration Stage:At this stage, the prospect develops a sizeable understanding of the problem and is in a phase of evelaution of the alternatives which would help him/her address the problem. In this stage, the prospect also gives due consideration to the time, effort and money involved in each of the alternatives. Online marketing helps the sales representatives tailor the brand to suit to the 'best fit' criteria of the prospect. This is done via influencing online perception of the brand as well as that of competitors. So a prospect facing the problem of blackheads would have explored all alternatives ranging fromm cosmetic surgery to simple home remeadies. A brand of face wash addressing the problem, might possibly position itself as economic, effective and natural way of tackling the problem.

Decision Stage: At this stage, prospect is in the phase of purchase decision whereby he/ she evaluates the various channels which offer the brand, their respective advantages and disadvantages as well as the financing option available in each of the channels. At this stage, the prospect also evaluates the competitor brands as well as the incentives available by them. Online marketing helps the sales representatives with offering the Unique Selling Proposition to the prospect, thereby helping the brand position itself distinctly in the minds of the buyer. Therefore, the brand of face wash might partner itself with the online marketplace like Amazon, Big Basket to offer bundle pricing to the prospect. The brand's online marketing efforts coupled with the marketplace's marketing efforts serve as a compelling proposition especially on the convenience and pricing parameters.

4. **Online marketing is measurable:** One of biggest advantage of online marketing, for a marketer is the measurability of every penny across all avenues. The marketer is able to get specific numbers on the impressions, views, clicks, time spent on a particular web page. The marketers can deploy real time digital analytics software to see the number of pages visited, devices from which their website is being checked out as well as the geographical region from where the prospect has accessed thee website. Online marketing analytics helps to understand the patterns of prospect behviour as well as the trends which influence it. For example, a boutique shop may print pamphlets/leaflets to raise its brand awareness amongst the neighbourhood. After the distribution of the leaflets, it has no clue on the number of leaflets which have been actually read and not discarded as a waste paper. Conversely, if the same leaflet was displayed on a social media platform or its very own website, the boutique marketer would have the exact number of people who had viewed it and downloaded it. In addition to the same, the use of cookies on the website will help in generating qualified leads.

Let us understand the online marketing analysis in detail.

Online Marketing Analysis:

As discussed earlier, online marketing analysis helps to understand the performance of digital channel which could include website, social media channels, blogs, SEO and affiliate websites. The analysis helps to understand the relationship between different marketing channels as well as the measurement of the revenue earned by each. It also provides an understanding of the buyer`s interaction with the various marketing efforts.

Relationship between different marketing channels: *Online analytics provides a holistic view of the interaction and impact of the marketing initiatives taken across the marketing channels. For example, if a brand undertakes the communication campaign executed through blog and email, online analytics helps a marketer understand the effectiveness of each channel in terms of number of clicks, downloads made by prospects.*

Measurement of the revenue: *Online analytics when combined with customer relationship management platform creates a closed loop data, which helps to determine the revenue contribution of each channel. This helps one to determine the key channels contributing to conversion and revenue generation.*

***Understanding of the buyer`s interaction:*** *Online analytics helps marketers understand how prospects interact with various channels and initiatives. For example, it helps them understand how the prospect landed on the brand`s website ie. Through search engine (Google, Bing,) or through social media platforms or through blog, or through email. A full stack online analytics helps one with valuable intelligence and help in understanding the trends and leads. These insights prove extremely valuable in designing marketing activities for various stages of the prospects decision making journey.*

Artificial Intelligence

In our professional life, we have all worked on excel. We have also worked on large excel sheets containing ten thousands of rows and maybe more than 100 coloums. We have resorted to basic excel functions like addition, subtraction, division and multiplication for understanding the data contained in the excel sheet. Some of these sheets required analysis which helped managers with insights. This was arrived using higher level of excel functions like pivot table, VLOOKUP, HLOOKUP etc. However, with the customer transending into fast paced life in the online space and being increasingly influenced by offline factors too, the data has no longer remained numeric. It has now transformed to being alpha numeric and textual. Higher level softwares like SPSS AMOS, SmartPLS have enabled to understand the data but nonetheless these softwares also had limmitations in analysisng the sentiments expressed by the customers in their textual messages, voice messages, podcasts, videos, vlogs etc.

It is here that professionals have resorted to large language models and neural networks. Machine Learning is often considered the evolutionary step towards artificial intelligence. The growth in the adoption of machine learning and artificial intelligence can be assessed from the fact that artificial intelligence is forecasted to add 15.7 trillion dollors to the world economy. The market for artificial intelligence products and services is forecasted to be worth 7.8 billion dollors with Industrials & Automotive, Healthcare, Retail and CPG. BFSI and Agri-tech leading in application of artificial intelligence[8].

The world's business development can't move further without artificial intelligence (AI). Artificial intelligence is predicted to contribute $15.7 trillion to the world economy by 2030, surpassing the combined GDP of China and India. India is home to the world's third-largest pool of AI talent, and the country is poised to become a global leader in the AI revolution. Investments in India's AI capabilities are predicted to reach $881 million by 2023, rising at a CAGR of 30.8%. [34]

The Indian artificial intelligence market, which is expected to reach a value of $7.8 billion by 2025, would be supported by the country's expanding semiconductor sector. According to projections, four end-user sectors—industrials and automotive, healthcare, retail, and consumer packaged goods—will account for 60% of artificial intelligence's gross value added (GVA) to India's GDP by 2025. New and exciting areas for AI applications include BFSI and Agri-tech[30].

With almost half of the population working in agriculture and contributing 18% to GDP, it's clear that agriculture plays a significant role in India's economy[42]. If we want to increase crop yields while decreasing waste, we must optimize the agricultural supply chain. Intello Labs' groundbreaking horticultural commerce service, Pramaan Exchange, uses computer vision and a large photo library to assess the quality of horticultural commodities. When compared to manual evaluations, which only achieve 70% accuracy, Pramaan's quality assaying system—which was initially developed for cardamom—achieves 95% accuracy. Since its introduction in 2021, this platform has allowed buyers and sellers to trade apples and onions in a flexible manner, resulting in a transaction value of over $600 million per year[31].

In the realm of financial technology, a well-known company is Razorpay, which uses artificial intelligence to make decisions. It can receive, process, and disperse payments for people and businesses alike, making it one of the primary payment gateways in India. As a precaution against fraud, Razorpay employs the artificial intelligence tool Third Watch. Whenever a modern customer books a cab, orders food or groceries online, or completes any kind of transaction, the Razorpay logo shows. Since its start, Razorpay has amassed $816 million in investment, and the company is now well-established. The journey taken by Razorpay shows how India can support and integrate AI-driven innovative companies into established and regulated markets[37].

One such AI application that is constructively disrupting a conventional industry is Sigtuple, a health-tech startup based in Bengaluru. Their one-of-a-kind gadgets streamline in-vitro diagnostic biological sample analysis[53]. Because of this, healthcare providers can diagnose patients much more quickly and at a far lower cost, and treatment can start much earlier. Binny Bansal and Accel Investors were among the seasoned investors that helped this firm raise almost $41 million over the course of five funding rounds. Healthcare technology driven by AI allows medical workers to serve a larger population more efficiently and with greater accuracy[35].

Furthermore, investors in all three examples highlighted thus far have realized that AI use cases, when tailored to India's specific geography, culture, and economic constraints, may generate enormous financial and social benefits. The growth of AI in India is dependent on identifying AI applications that decrease manual work while improving and streamlining critical business processes. These business transitions necessitate support from enterprise executives, an inventive talent pool, and a thriving business environment.

Staff members need to have experience in artificial intelligence (AI) as well as customer-centric skills like design thinking, problem-solving, and communication in order to build machine learning models, according to surveys of industry professionals. India could benefit from its position as the world's second-largest pool of artificial intelligence experts. Indian Institute of Science (IISc) in Bengaluru and the government of Karnataka have joined forces to create ARTPARK, a $100 million venture fund that would put money into companies that deal with artificial intelligence and robotics. This shows that educational institutions are already cognizant of this potential. As an example of industry-government partnership, ARTPARK researchers and HealthTech startup Analytix Niramai Health developed an AI model called XraySetu. They held the Innovation Summit 2022 to showcase the importance of 5G, AI, and Robotics to the Indian economy, and they are also keen on developing India's entire AI ecosystem[46].

The Indian Budget 2023–24 was another vehicle via which the federal government advanced this objective. In the proposed budget, the government laid out its plans to create three AI Centers of Excellence at prestigious universities. They had previously partnered with the trade group NASSCOM, which publishes papers, hosts events, and provides seminars, to build an AI platform. Responsible AI for Social Empowerment (get) was a startup event they organized to help AI firms get money and showcase their technologies.

Artifical Intelligence vs Machine Learning vs Deep Learning[33]:

Who thinks of which idea first? That's the age-old conundrum. While many people still don't understand what each of these terms means, data scientists and engineers have a firm grasp on the subject. A British naturalist named Charles Darwin proposed the idea of evolution. He had described evolution as the process of descent with modification, in which a species undergoes a single transformation that ultimately gives rise to a new species that shares an ancestor with Homosapiens. There is no intention for AI, ML, and Data Science to have separate narratives. Actually, mathematics is the very foundation upon which all of them rest. The title of "mother of artificial intelligence" was once held by Ada Covalace, among others. She made history by being the first to notice Babbage's Analytical Engines, a precursor to the modern computer that could follow rules to manipulate symbols other than numbers, including musical notes. On the other hand, John Mc Carthy is widely recognized as the pioneer of artificial intelligence. The field of artificial intelligence was co-founded by along with him, Alan Novell, Marvin Kindey, Alan Turing, and Herbert A. worked extensively on reinforcement learning, both supervised and unsupervised. In contrast, AI is a set of tools that allows computers to mimic human intelligence in areas such as understanding, interpretation, learning, and decision-making. The primary goal of artificial intelligence is to simulate human intelligence in machines. Conversely, data science aids AI and ML in understanding past data, seeing trends, and forecasting future outcomes. Data science, in contrast to artificial intelligence (AI), focuses on transforming insights into knowledge for improved decision-making. Taking a page out of consumer behavior studies' playbook, this is how a customer forms an opinion about his company's brand: from initial interest, through perception and understanding, to final decision-making.

Therefore, aspiring marketers should think about machine learning as a tool that may improve their understanding of customer behavior changes, which in turn can improve their brand's reputation among potential customers.

The use of AI can greatly benefit marketers by expanding their knowledge and comprehension of customer behavior. Meanwhile, data science helps marketers better grasp customer sentiment by providing in-depth insights into behavioral trends. Data science, in contrast to artificial intelligence, makes use of a variety of tools, including rigorous statistical methods, to get results.

Applications of AI, ML, Data Sciences in Marketing

The vast majority of machine learning uses center on enhancing quality through the mitigation of flaws. For instance, with the use of ML, AI, and Data Sciences, merchants may provide their customers with better inventory management and shipping options. With the use of voice recognition technology, smart gadgets may better meet client needs by delivering the best platter at the command of a word.

Improvements in illness detection and prompt medical intervention have a profound impact on the healthcare support system, ultimately leading to lifesaving outcomes. For instance, doctors can now see cancer in its earliest stages, even in tiny nodes, thanks to recent developments in AI and ML. Consequently, allowing for prompt action. Improvements in e-commerce site customer service are made possible by ML-driven breakthroughs in product recommendation. No less than first-rate cyber protection and fraud detection can be achieved through the integration of AI, ML, and data sciences. With improved pattern detection of the hackers, for instance, banks have been able to stop cyber scams.

Machine Learning (ML) and Marketing:

Machine learning impacts three aspects of marketing:

1. Customer segmentation: Segmenting the market is the first and most crucial step in developing a successful marketing plan. Nevertheless, marketers frequently err when it comes to segmentation, which ultimately derail any attempts at developing a successful marketing strategy. The use of ML software can greatly improve the efficacy and precision of the consumer segmentation process. On top of that, ML algorithms are useful for segment and pattern recognition. Marketers can participate in hyper segmentation with the help of the correct ML model, which allows them to personalize their marketing strategies. Marketers are able to improve customer relationship management and launch more successful campaigns thanks to this personalization, which enables them to produce material that is both highly relevant and tailored to the target audience.

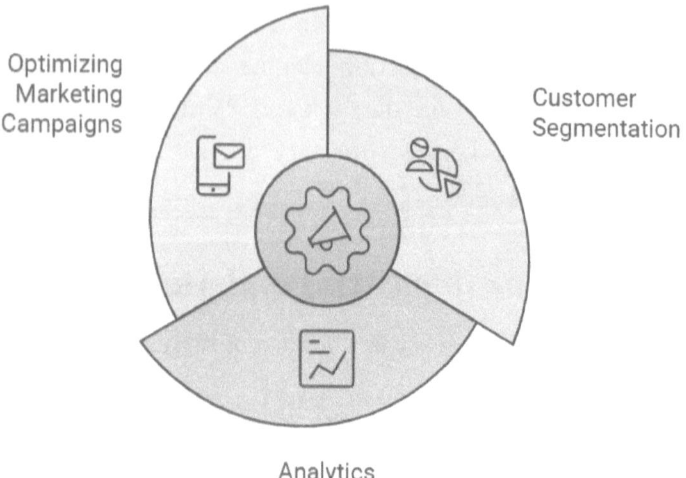

2. Analytics: Data is the new oil in today's corporate environment. Data management and analysis has become more important for marketing managers due to the rise of social media and internet marketing. The sheer size of a dataset can quickly become too much for a single individual to handle. Here, data administration and analysis are made easier with the help of a machine learning tool. Online reputation management and sales data processing are two areas that can benefit from machine learning algorithms. Plus, they're useful for predictive analytics and seeing intricate patterns.

3. Optimizing Marketing Campaign: It was challenging to forecast the success criteria for a product or brand launch marketing campaign before the advent of AI. However, with

the advent of AI and ML, data analytics and processing have been invaluable tools for marketers in reaching their target audiences. Additionally, ML software aids in automating marketing initiatives, which increases productivity, and in securing a larger return on investment.

Artificial Intelligence (AI) and Marketing:

Artificial Intelligence impacts three aspects of marketing:

1. Functions as a Digital Assistant for customers engaged in the deliberation and research phases of the purchasing cycle: Marketers may use AI to target adverts to specific consumers, while consumers can use it to find the best brand for their needs. Through the use of chat, phone, video, and even cobrowsing, bots powered by artificial intelligence may improve brand connection with customers.

2. Streamline Sales Process: AI has the potential to revolutionize sales by leveraging extensive personal data, such as real-time geolocation information, to generate highly tailored product or service recommendations. Towards the end of the trip, AI can aid in upselling and cross-selling items and reduce the likelihood of customers leaving their online shopping carts unfinished. In order to boost food delivery orders in Mexico City during high traffic hours, Burger King's Traffic Jam Whopper campaign employed artificial intelligence. Daily delivery orders in Mexico City increased by 63% throughout the trial period, and the campaign saw a notable uptick in sales during busy traffic times.

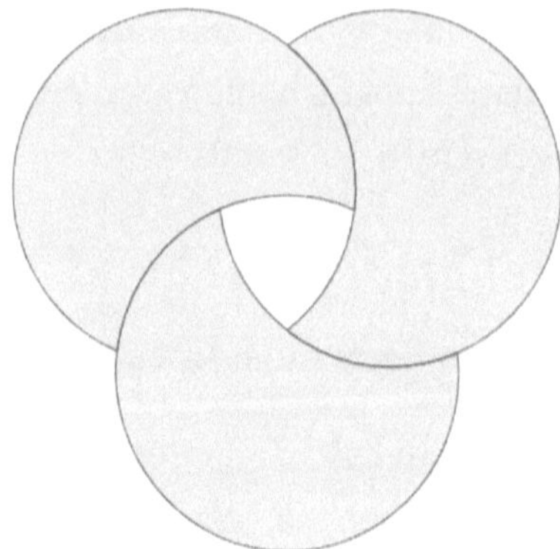

1. Streamline After -Sales Process: Among the several providers of AI-enabled customer support agents are Amelia (formerly IPsoft) and Interactions, to name a few. In comparison to human operators, these bots can manage varying volumes of requests more efficiently and are available 24/7 to triage customers' concerns. This bot can be instructed to forward more complex inquiries to a human agent if the consumer needs help with things like appointment scheduling or tracking their order. In certain scenarios, artificial intelligence (AI) can augment human salespeople by analyzing client tone and providing multiple responses, directing agents to better fulfill clients' expectations, or even suggesting that a supervisor step in.

Data Sciences and Marketing:

New data science trends reflect the growing prospects for enterprises in product creation, consumer value, and customer service, among other areas.

1. **Channel Optimization:** Age, location, and gender are some of the conventional demographics that businesses have used to make assumptions about their customers. Marketers and businesses gain very little insight into consumers and their wants from these specifics. Affinity (or market basket) analysis is one data science tool that can help companies better understand their customers and how to advertise to them. If the customer's social media behavior is thoroughly investigated, a story may be uncovered by the links that are found. You may see where your ads and content might have reached your target customer on sites like Pinterest, Instagram, and YouTube through this pathway if you're not currently doing it.

2. **Customer Segmentation:** You need to know what your customers want before you can craft a marketing plan that will work. Although every customer is unique, marketing campaigns can be more effectively targeted by using methods to categorize customers' goals, requirements, and issues. Customers can be categorized based on their location, purchasing history, and how they navigate your website. Using targeted machine learning approaches, data scientists can discover valuable target audiences and the products that would appeal to them. This may guide your content strategy, optimize your channels, and help you target leads more effectively.

3. **Lead targeting and advanced lead scoring:** The most challenging part of digital marketing, according to most people, is timing your outreach to the proper potential customers. Data science and machine learning make customer analytics much easier to implement. Through sophisticated statistical analysis of your marketing data in conjunction with insights from data libraries, data scientists can predict when and where specific items and promotions will have the highest level of interest. Look at things like the consumer's word choice when interacting with you, the qualities of the client category they belong to, and earlier behaviors of similar customers to evaluate the prospective worth of each lead or customer. Instead of spending money on marketing based on speculation and trial and error, you can use this method. Any new goods or services you decide to develop, as well as future marketing decisions, will be informed by the efficacy of each prediction algorithm. When combined with a machine learning model, lead targeting can transform this procedure into an automated, self-improving system.

4. **Real-time interaction and Analytics:** Businesses can fall behind the competition if they wait too long to acquire data that can help them make better marketing decisions. At a potentially pivotal moment for customer conversion, real-time analytics allow organizations to track and analyze consumer behavior in real-time, giving valuable, actionable insights. Saving money and avoiding wasted marketing efforts is possible with real-time analytics since they provide a faster response time when your target market changes. There are two main applications of real-time analytics in marketing, which are:

- giving out personalized promotions and discounts to chosen consumers as they shop online or in-store;

- and, learning when and why sales are successful or unsuccessful by observing consumer behavior

5. **Content Strategy:** Sometimes it feels like you're shooting in the dark while trying to come up with a content marketing plan that can attract new prospects. You may get a lot of engagement and sales from your content, but without analytics and statistics to back it up, it can be hard to tell what your customers really want. In this case, data science becomes useful. Data science techniques like serial testing makes testing—which is still essential for understanding your content's quality—the most effective and least time-exhaustive option by utilizing an unsupervised machine learning algorithm. Small aspects like word choice and color can be fine-tuned with the help of serial testing. Then, you can use techniques like time-series forecasting to figure out when these creative decisions will work best across all platforms, so you can show fully optimized content to the right people at the right time.

6. **Sentiment Analysis:** It is critical to work on building a good name for your company or product. The first impression your customers get of your business, whether through social media or your website, can have a significant impact on their opinion of you even before they use your service. Reviews or reactions made by other users often influence this attitude. By appealing to your customers' sentiments using sentiment analysis, you can take command of your reputation. This data analysis can be done manually, but machine learning techniques make it much faster and more effective. To give

every social media post a score depending on the responses in the comments area, specific words might be given positive, neutral, or negative ratings. Using speech-to-text analytics, the same principle may be extended to phone conversations, Google reviews, and email correspondence as well. You may use this information to pinpoint the areas of customer service that are falling short and identify which products, services, or social media marketing campaigns are attracting the attention you want from your target audience.

7. **Maintaining customer loyalty:** Instead of focusing entirely on customer acquisition, your marketing money can be better spent on customer loyalty and improving the lifetime value of your average customer. With the use of data science and ML models, companies can find three potential ways to boost customer loyalty:

    - the optimal course of action or offer for every consumer as they navigate your website or use your product;

    - the potential customer's reaction to a given situation;

    - the issue at hand in the event that a client cancels their account

Following the discovery of these three elements, you will be able to address numerous issues that may be discouraging customers from returning, establish automated recommendations for previous clients, and anticipate the optimal course of action in the event that a particular contact materializes. Marketing to a consumer who has previously had a positive experience with you is easier and more cost-effective than marketing to a "cold" lead because their customer data is readily available.

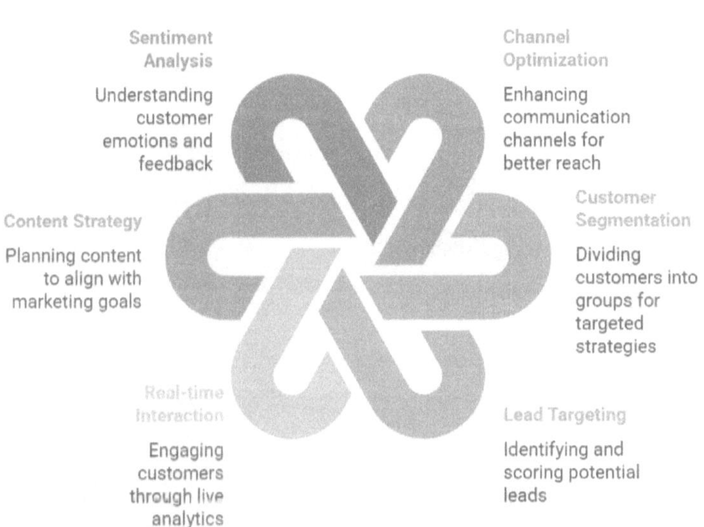

8. **Predictive analytics:** To foretell potential outcomes influencing your company or your client, predictive analytics include a number of machine learning models and algorithms (and occasionally AI in general). The proliferation of IoT devices has resulted in an unprecedented amount of data available for use in making forecasts. As a result, with the correct framework in place, these predictions can now be more precise than ever before. Companies can benefit from predictive analytics by doing the following:

- Distribution of material to the appropriate audiences;

- Targeting customers with a reduced churn rate and/or better potential lifetime value;

- Find out how well digital ads are doing before they go live ;

- Make good use of up-sell and cross-sell opportunities.

9. **Recommendation engines:** A strong predictive analytics system is the foundation upon which recommendation engines rest. The recommendation engine comes in two varieties:

- collaborative filtering

- and content-based filtering

Whatever the product category, a collaborative filtering-based recommendation engine will use the buying habits of other consumers to provide product suggestions. The content-based filtering recommendation engine takes the product category and description into account more thoroughly, allowing it to provide more relevant product pairings. The two varieties of recommendation engines are not without their drawbacks. Instead of upselling, content-based filters will suggest items that are extremely similar to the customer's current wants, and collaborative filters may suggest products that don't meet those criteria at all. As a result, the majority of companies employ a hybrid approach, proposing products according to kind, description, and previous success with clients who are similar to themselves.

10. **Marketing budget optimization:** Data science has as its overriding objective the maximum of the utilization of the marketing budget that your organization has available to it to the greatest extent possible. When your company maximizes the timing and targeting of product promotions, it can save money that would have been spent on marketing

strategies that are useless. You should be able to construct an automatic marketing plan that covers all the bases if you follow any of the processes that have been stated above. This includes conducting research on your target demographic and predicting how the weather will affect product sales. **Regression analysis:** Regression analysis is like a reliable magnifying glass that helps us uncover the hidden patterns in data, like setting out on an exciting detective adventure. Imagine a graph that shows the complex interaction of multiple variables in the context of marketing. By analyzing the relationship between independent and dependent variables, this statistical behemoth helps us zero in on the factors that matter most for propelling change. As we run the numbers, regression analysis becomes our trusted companion, shedding light on the variables that determine consumer actions. With these insights at your disposal, you can develop audience-specific strategies and make data-driven marketing decisions with long-term impact.

11. **Price recommendations for retail:** Within the retail sector, which is always evolving, data science has shown to be an extremely significant asset. Businesses are provided with the capacity to confidently and accurately manage the ever-changing waves of pricing strategies as a result of this. Machine learning and sentiment analysis have the potential to give merchants with invaluable knowledge regarding the reactions and preferences of customers with whom they interact. Their method, which is driven by data, enables them to calculate ideal prices that appeal to their target demographic. This, in turn, increases the level of satisfaction experienced by customers and leads to increased revenues. In order for businesses to prosper in the cutthroat retail market

of today, they need to grab the opportunity given by data science. This is necessary if they want to withstand the digital revolution and remain ahead of the competition.

Summary of Benefits of using Data Science in marketing

It could be a mistake to exclude data science from your marketing plan in today's fast-paced, digital world. Data science's benefits will quickly outweigh the costs of recruitment and initial setup. **These benefits include:**

- Spend less time and energy on marketing strategies that don't work

- Raise the lifetime value of a customer

- Focus on the most valued customers

- Get the most out of your digital advertising spend;

- Increase conversions by using up-and cross-selling strategies;

- Learn from client feedback quickly;

- Forecast future product and service popularity

Case Studies of Companies employing AI, ML and Data Sciences to drive performance:

DaVita: A kidney care company drove 42% more job application[25]

DaVita is an American healthcare provider. The medical treatment of renal problems is the company's main focus. The organization has treated 200,000 patients over 2200 centers. The accomplishment would not have been possible without the 60,000 hardworking individuals that the organization refers to as teammates. The company's leadership understood the need of attracting talented people to ensure high-quality patient care. According to the company's experience, the management's choice of patient care professionals has a direct impact on the quality of treatment patients receive. Therefore, it was crucial to employ competent medical practitioners, such as nurses and doctors. Nevertheless, DaVita encountered difficulty in luring talent due to escalating competition in the labor market and shrinking budgets. Despite the fact that social media is more commonly associated with marketing and recruiting with human resources, the teams at DaVita came to the realization that they might improve their strategy by working together.

The teams first determined that highlighting the wonderful work environment at DaVita is the most effective strategy to recruit healthcare professionals and nurses. Innovation, a friendly atmosphere, excellent perks, and numerous career prospects were the four pillars of content that they used to emphasize this. According to David Tauchen, the Director of Communications,

Owned Content, and Social Media for DaVita, the company also realized that bragging on branded social media pages wouldn't yield the desired outcomes. He knew that as per research, people trusted the opinions of individuals much more than those of brands. Staff members at DaVita were encouraged to convey the company's true character—a dedication to providing excellent patient care—by opening up about their own experiences on the job. Their stories reached more people because of their use of employees' networks. Hundreds of teammates will shared every post to their personal networks.

However, it was going to be difficult to maintain a consistent story with around 200 talent acquisition partners and ambassadors participating. The risks associated with noncompliance and brand safety were additional considerations.

Providing ambassadors with compelling content to share

To ensure the success of this plan, the teams recognized the necessity for a straightforward and scalable method for their ambassadors to disseminate pre-approved, brand-safe content. The team used Hootsuite Amplify which is an employee advocacy tool that facilitates the safe sharing of company social media postings by staff members, increasing brand recognition and reaching a wider audience. Kristin Landreth, the Employment Brand Content Manager at DaVita, elucidated that simplicity was crucial for uptake. The Amplify platform made it easier for acquisition team to effortlessly select stories they wished to disseminate and publish on their social media channels. The Amplify platform ensured that the stories were brand aligned as well as approved. Thus, the team could use the content in its entirety.

Facilitating team members' ease of use is, of course, only one consideration. The content's compellingness to spread was of equal importance.

Jenny Nailling, DaVita's communications manager, put a premium on featuring motivational stories about individual teammates and the role the company played in their professional development. The team wanted to share the authentic story of DaVita and demonstrate what life could look like as a DaVita teammate. At this point, 200 ambassadors from various teams are spreading the word about DaVita's achievements on social media. Plus, those stories were being safely and easily shared with a larger audience of potential recruits using Hootsuite Amplify.

The Result:

Hootsuite Amplify was a huge hit for DaVita, and it's easy to see why: it made sharing motivational stories a breeze. The campaign sawmore than 24,000 shares Ad value comparable to almost $1.5 million The initiative has seen an 80% sustained adoption rate, a 136% increase in traffic from LinkedIn to their career site, and a 27% rise in job applications via social media year over year.

The team also claimed that DaVita's career website receives significantly better quality traffic. But the most remarkable thing is how the program's results are closely related to the recruitment team's long-term objectives. DaVita is now considering expanding the program to attract more ambassadors due to its success.

Airbnb

If you want to see how data science can revolutionize marketing, go no further than Airbnb. They recruited a data scientist when the company was just seven individuals strong, and that decision was crucial to their tremendous success. With the expansion of the corporation, data science has taken on a more complex role, with experts analyzing data for all divisions. Since the founder saw data science's growth-inducing potential, it has been a top priority, ensuring that opportunities and challenges at all levels have been thoroughly investigated. Using in-house development tools like Airflow and Airpal, hosts and customers can now learn from each other, and data power is at the hands of any employee.

Netflix

Keeping subscribers engaged and coming back for more is a top priority for content subscription services like Netflix. This is precisely why Netflix has its recommendation engine, which uses user viewing habits to suggest new movies and TV shows. Subscribing users month after month is the ultimate goal, even though the first-hand effect is enlightening, useful, and personal.

Spotify

Like Netflix, Spotify wants to keep its subscribers by constantly inventing fresh methods to find music. Given the two kinds of content, the most obvious distinction between Spotify and Netflix is the enormous volume of content that Spotify delivers. Therefore, it is far more difficult to manually seek for new music that you will appreciate on Spotify than it is to find a new film or series on Netflix. In an effort to address this issue, the Discover Weekly playlist is one such endeavor. The listening habits of comparable users will be used to create a personalized playlist for each user every Monday. In a similar vein, Spotify's Release Radar keeps users apprised of new music from artists Spotify knows they appreciate, while the Daily Mix combines the user's existing music library with recommendations for new songs to listen to. These concepts ensure that every user's account is always current, fascinating, and fresh, even when they don't do anything.

Facebook

At Facebook, data science is approached from multiple angles. Thousands of business owners use their platform to market, and they offer marketing tools and insights in addition to their own analytics that they monitor and act upon. Strategies that really help their clients succeed are absolutely necessary. With the help of machine learning models, Facebook is able to distribute marketing campaigns to its customers efficiently, analyze the success of those ads, and provide its own marketing staff with insights and tools to better assist business owners.

Google

In the same vein as Facebook, Google's goal is to provide its business-owning customers with a substantial return on investment. Since most SMBs do not employ data scientists full-time, they will have to depend on Google to handle all of their marketing analytics on their behalf. Simplifying and making the metrics as easy to read as possible is the goal. While Google's in-house marketing team targets the most likely buyers, the company offers business owners just the most useful tools to build their marketing campaigns and track their success.

Exposition:
Part II

Types of Artificial Intelligence (AI)[50]

Artificial intelligence (AI) technology is something you've encountered if you've ever used a chatbot, Apple's Face ID, or Amazon's Alexa.

Ongoing AI research and development encompasses a wide range of topics, most of which fall into distinct categories. Rather than revealing a taxonomy, these categories provide light on a narrative that may teach us about the history, current state, and future of artificial intelligence.

Here are seven categories of AI and what they entail, as well as future predictions for the technology.

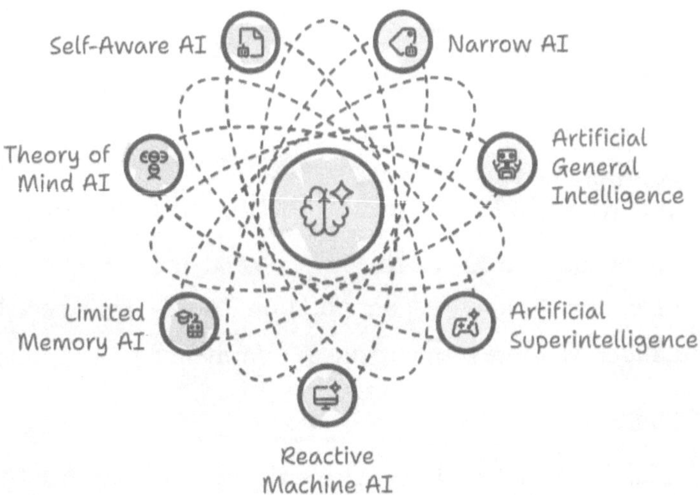

1. **Narrow AI:** AI that is programmed to do very specific tasks but can't learn on its own.

2. **Artificial General Intelligence:** AI that is made to learn, think, and do things at the same level as people.

3. **Artificial Superintelligence:** Artificial intelligence that can outstrip human intelligence and capability.

4. **Reactive Machine AI:** Artificial intelligence that can react instantly to the world around it but lacks the ability to learn or remember anything.

5. **Limited Memory AI:** Artificial intelligence with the ability to learn and retain new information for application in future situations.

6. **Theory of Mind AI:** Artificial intelligence capable of seeing and reacting to human emotions, in addition to executing the functions of restricted memory systems.

7. **Self-Aware AI:** Artificial intelligence capable of recognizing the emotions of others, possessing self-awareness, and exhibiting human-level intelligence; the ultimate phase of AI development.

Capability-Based Types of Artificial Intelligence

AI can be categorized into three types based on learning methods and the extent of knowledge application: Narrow AI, General AI, and Super AI. Here is the pertinent information on each item.

1. **Narrow AI**

Narrow AI, referred to as artificial narrow intelligence (ANI) or weak AI, pertains to AI systems engineered to perform highly specific tasks or directives. ANI technologies are designed to excel in a singular cognitive function and lack the ability to autonomously acquire skills beyond their predetermined framework. They frequently employ machine learning and neural network methods to accomplish these designated tasks. Natural language processing exemplifies restricted AI, as it can identify and react to voice commands, yet is incapable of executing tasks beyond this scope. Examples of narrow AI encompass image recognition software, autonomous vehicles, and AI virtual assistants.

2. Artificial General Intelligence (AGI)

Artificial general intelligence (AGI), sometimes known as general AI or strong AI, refers to AI capable of learning, reasoning, and executing a diverse array of tasks akin to human abilities. The objective of developing artificial general intelligence is to build computers capable of executing multipurpose activities and serving as lifelike, equally intelligent aides to humans in daily life.

Although currently under development, the foundation of artificial general intelligence may be established using technologies such as supercomputers, quantum hardware, and generative AI models like ChatGPT.

3. Artificial Superintelligence

Artificial superintelligence (ASI), or super AI, is a concept rooted in science fiction. It is posited that upon attaining general intelligence, AI will rapidly acquire knowledge and skills, surpassing those of humanity. ASI would serve as the foundational technology for fully self-aware AI and other autonomous robots. The notion also underpins the prevalent media narrative of "AI takeovers." At this juncture, it is merely conjecture. As per Dave Rogenmoser, CEO of Jasper, Artificial superintelligence will possess human-like intelligence and will significantly surpass human capabilities in all endeavors.

Functionality-Based Types of Artificial Intelligence

Functionality refers to the manner in which an AI employs its learning capabilities to process data, respond to stimuli, and interact with its environment. Consequently, AI can be categorized into four functional categories:

4. **Reactive Machine AI**

Reactive machines are fundamentally reactionary. They can address urgent demands and tasks; nevertheless, they lack the ability to retain memory, learn from prior events, or enhance their functionality through such encounters. Furthermore, reactive machines can just react to a restricted array of inputs. Reactive machines are the most basic category of artificial intelligence. In fact, reactive robots are effective for executing fundamental autonomous tasks, such as screening spam from email inboxes or suggesting things based on buying history. However, reactive AI is incapable of using prior knowledge or executing more intricate tasks.

Reactive Machine AI Examples

- IBM Deep Blue: IBM's reactive AI system, Deep Blue, successfully interpreted real-time signals to defeat Russian chess grandmaster Garry Kasparov in a chess match in 1997.

- Netflix Recommendation Engine: Media services such as Netflix frequently employ AI-driven recommendation systems that analyze a user's viewing history to identify and propose content they are most inclined to watch next.

5. Limited Memory AI

Limited memory Artificial intelligence can retain historical data and utilize it for predictive analysis. This indicates that it actively constructs a constrained, ephemeral knowledge base and executes actions predicated on that information. Limited memory AI fundamentally relies on deep learning, which emulates the operations of neurons in the human brain. This enables a machine to assimilate data from events and "learn" from them, so enhancing the precision of its operations over time. The restricted memory model constitutes the predominant framework for AI applications nowadays. It can be utilized in a wide array of contexts, ranging from smaller-scale applications like chatbots to sophisticated use cases such as autonomous vehicles.

Limited Memory AI Examples

- Chatbots and virtual assistants are types of limited memory AI that employ deep learning to imitate conversations between people. As users engage increasingly with these systems, they assimilate data and retain information about the user, enabling them to deliver pertinent and customized responses.

- Self-Driving Cars: Autonomous vehicles consistently monitor and analyze environmental data in their vicinity while navigating roadways. This enables them to anticipate when to turn, halt, or evade an obstacle.

6. Theory of Mind AI

Theory of Mind pertains to the notion of AI that can recognize and interpret the emotions of others. The phrase, derived from psychology, refers to humans' capacity to discern the emotions of others and anticipate subsequent actions based on that insight. Theory of Mind has not yet been fully achieved and is the next significant milestone in the advancement of AI. Theory of Mind may yield numerous beneficial transformations in the technology sector, although it concurrently presents inherent hazards. Given the intricacy of emotional cues, it would require considerable time for AI systems to master their interpretation, perhaps resulting in significant errors throughout the learning phase. Some individuals additionally apprehend that whenever technologies can react to emotional cues alongside situational ones, it may lead to the automation of certain occupations.

Theory of Mind AI Example

Rafael Tena, a senior AI researcher at Acrisure, an insurance firm, presented an example to demonstrate how an effective Theory of Mind application will transform the technology. A self-driving automobile is likely to outperform a human driver most of the time due to its inability to commit typical human errors. However, if you, as a driver, are aware that your neighbor's child frequently plays near the roadway after school, you will automatically reduce your speed while approaching that neighbor's driveway—an action that an AI vehicle with basic limited memory would be incapable of doing.

7. Self-Aware AI

Self-Aware AI refers to artificial intelligence that exhibits self-awareness. Known as the AI point of singularity, self-aware AI is a leap beyond theory of mind and constitutes one of the paramount objectives in AI advancement. It is believed that upon achieving self-aware AI, these robots will surpass human control, as they will possess the ability to perceive the emotions of others and possess self-awareness.

Self-Aware AI Example

One of the most renowned examples is Sophia, a robot created by the robotics firm Hanson Robotics. Although not genuinely self-aware, Sophia's sophisticated utilization of contemporary AI technologies offers a preview of AI's possible self-aware future. The future presents both potential and peril, prompting debate regarding the ethical implications of developing sentient AI.

AI in Marketing[2]

Artificial intelligence is set to assume a progressively vital role in marketing and sales. Trends indicate an increasing dependence on AI for prompt customer service interactions, predictive market analysis, and highly tailored content creation. The continuous advancement of AI technology will certainly furnish marketers with new tools and alternatives to foster innovation and attain progressively remarkable results.

Current State of AI in Marketing

In the dynamic age of digital transformation, the field of marketing is significantly influenced by the advancements of Artificial Intelligence (AI). Artificial intelligence has undoubtedly transformed the marketing industry, enhancing its efficiency, personalization, and interactivity to unprecedented levels.

AI-Driven Personalization

Personalization is essential for efficient marketing, and AI has significantly enhanced this capability. AI categorizes audiences by their behavior, interests, and demographic characteristics, allowing marketers to customize their strategies to meet specific requirements. The implementation of recommendation engines, driven by AI algorithms, is a notable aspect of AI-enhanced customization. These engines tailor items or services to each consumer, hence increasing the likelihood of conversions. Artificial intelligence has revolutionized email marketing as well, Through the analysis of prior interactions, AI can forecast optimal periods for email dispatch, the most impactful subject lines, and the content types that would elicit the better engagement rates.

Predictive Analytics

Predictive analytics is beneficial for anticipating future results by utilizing past data and analytical methods. AI models can analyze vast quantities of data to discern patterns and trends that assist in forecasting customer behavior, market dynamics, and potential hazards. This predictive ability enables firms to formulate strategies successfully, foresee client requirements, and maintain a competitive edge in the market.

Chatbots and Social Bots

AI-driven chatbots have transformed the customer service sector by facilitating round-the-clock client support. They can manage many inquiries concurrently, therefore conserving time and resources. Equipped with natural language processing abilities, these bots can comprehend and address client inquiries in a conversational format. Conversely, social bots are explicitly engineered for social media sites. They oversee multiple responsibilities, including disseminating updates, replying to communications, monitoring mentions, and evaluating sentiment. This aids brands in sustaining a consistent social media presence and proactive client interaction.

AI in SEO and Content Strategy

The significance of AI in influencing SEO and content strategy is crucial. AI-driven solutions may assess keywords, detect content deficiencies, propose themes that engage the audience, and assist in generating superior content. They can evaluate website performance, enhance on-page SEO elements, and recommend enhancements. The capabilities of AI in automated content production and curation are remarkable.

Certain AI technologies may produce optimized blogs, social media posts, advertisement copy, and even lengthy content within minutes, thereby conserving hours of manual labor. Artificial intelligence has significantly transformed the marketing landscape. AI's contributions span customization, analytics, chatbots, and content strategy, and are poised to expand significantly in the forthcoming years. The incorporation of AI has enhanced marketing strategies and provided consumers with a more engaging and personalized experience. AI and marketing appear to be an ideal combination in the digital realm.

Emerging Trends in AI Marketing

We are now in an era characterized by unparalleled digital advancement, where conventional marketing techniques are being dismantled and reconstructed using the power of Artificial Intelligence (AI). As digital marketers adapt to AI breakthroughs, four emerging patterns have gained prominence. This encompasses Augmented Reality/Virtual Reality (AR/VR) support in marketing, sophisticated SEO strategies, influencer network evaluations, and automated content generation.

AR/VR Support in Marketing

Introduced to the marketing arena by the technologically adept millennial demographic, AR/VR technology is transforming the consumer experience. Its captivating allure is a remarkable achievement in engaging customers, captivating them like never before. Envision navigating a virtual store, selecting items from digital shelves, or experimenting with furniture to assess its appearance in your personal space; this exemplifies the marketing potential that AR/VR currently provides. Businesses are experiencing increased client interaction and, as a result, elevated conversion rates due to this trend.

Advanced SEO Techniques

Search Engine Optimization (SEO) is an indispensable element of every digital marketing plan. The advancement of SEO strategies has considerably intensified its influence. Innovative methods, including AI-driven keyword optimization, predictive SEO, voice search optimization, and algorithmic content audits, have recently gained prominence. These sophisticated approaches are swiftly transforming the digital marketing scene, ensuring enhanced and more effective search engine presence.

Influencer Network Analysis

Influencer marketing, often considered the most human aspect of digital marketing, has also been enhanced by the influence of AI. Influencer network analysis, an emerging technology, employs Artificial Intelligence to scrutinize extensive datasets and eliminate extraneous information, thereby uncovering potentially important influencers. This research considers aspects including follower interaction rates, engagement quality, and content relevancy, ensuring that organizations connect with influencers that correspond optimally with their brand and target audience.

Automated Content Creation

Another domain in which AI excels is content production. With the emergence of sophisticated algorithms and machine learning, AI is now capable of producing blog entries, social media updates, and extensive material. Leveraging structured data, these AI systems may generate well-articulated, pertinent, and distinctly original content, precisely aligned with the tastes of the target audience. Beyond merely conserving time, automated content creation can yield essential insights into user preferences, enhancing future content development.

The convergence of AI with digital marketing is a nexus of innovation, offering exceptional customer engagement and a transformative reconfiguration of marketing techniques. The current era is exhilarating for the profession as AI persistently shapes and enhances the effects of digital marketing, uncovering promising prospects for both enterprises and consumers. With AI supporting their tactics, marketers may anticipate enhanced understanding of their audiences and improved targeting capabilities, so augmenting the overall efficacy of their efforts.

Predictions for AI in Marketing[49]

In a short span, the synergy of artificial intelligence and marketing has fundamentally altered the corporate landscape, yielding remarkable advancements that were formerly inconceivable. As we rapidly approach the future, let us explore the significant transformations that AI is expected to introduce in the field of marketing.

    a. *Increased Automation:* Predictions on the role of AI in marketing by 2024 often center on the importance of automation. To keep up with the trends and devote more time to strategic planning and creative pursuits, more and more firms are seeing the benefits of automating mundane processes. Automated email marketing campaigns, chatbots to answer consumer questions, and predictive analytics to understand consumer behavior are all valuable tools that will likely become quite popular. It would appear that, with AI's easy incorporation, our creativity is the only limit to the amount of marketing automation.

b. *Mobile Marketing:* Experts anticipate a dramatic change towards mobile marketing, driven in large part by AI, due to the indisputable importance of mobile devices in our daily lives. Artificial intelligence (AI) may improve mobile user experiences in a variety of ways, including location-based marketing and voice search optimization. When it comes to developing marketing plans, this technology will play a crucial part in helping firms interact with their audiences on the devices they prefer.

c. *Hyper-Personalization:* While the idea of personalization isn't new to marketing, artificial intelligence is taking it to a whole new level. Think about this: computer programs that learn each user's habits, tastes, likes, and dislikes in order to provide suggestions and communications that are uniquely suited to them. Experts believe that AI will revolutionize client interactions by moving beyond simple "recommended for you" tags.

d. *AI and Blockchain Integration:* Marketers now have access to a potent, perceptive tool thanks to the combination of AI's learning capabilities with the immutability of blockchain technology. Marketing tactics that are more open and responsible are likely to become more popular. More targeted advertising, higher levels of consumer trust, and better data privacy could result from combining blockchain technology with AI by the year 2024.

While these forecasts do provide a fascinating glimpse into the future, there are several obstacles to overcome before implementing AI in marketing. If companies want to make the most of the AI marketing revolution, they must put resources into learning about and implementing these technologies.

Impact of AI on Marketing Job Roles:

Artificial Intelligence is at the helm as technology continues to sail into uncharted territory of progress. The revolutionary potential of AI is already causing an intriguing transformation in the marketing industry. Let's examine the effects of AI on marketing jobs in more detail.

Expansion of Skill Sets

There is no denying the truth of AI's incorporation into marketing. It has pushed marketers to embrace data analysis and intelligence-based automation, expanding their skill sets. Here are some of the AI-enhanced marketing tools that are causing a stir:

- **Data Analysis:** It will be anticipated by the employers that the marketers decipher intricate data patterns and turn them into plans.

- **Machine Learning Basics:** It has become increasingly necessary to have a basic understanding of machine learning technologies. Understanding the operation of AI algorithms can help with strategic planning, even if one isn't programming them.

- **Understanding of AI tools:** An advantage would be expertise with marketing tools that use artificial intelligence to simplify operations, such as chatbots to communicate with customers and platforms that use AI to curate content.

Reshaping of Marketing Strategies

AI has revolutionized the way marketers approach their strategies. Now that it's possible to automate the hitherto labor-intensive process of tailored advertising, we can achieve more targeted and lucrative outcomes. A fresh take on marketing responsibilities is required in light of these strategy rethinkings. For instance, in today's market, marketers are expected to excel at:

- Creating individualized programs: Making efficient use of AI capabilities to provide individualized programs

- Harnessing AI-powered predictive analytics to optimize the customer journey and improve the customer experience.

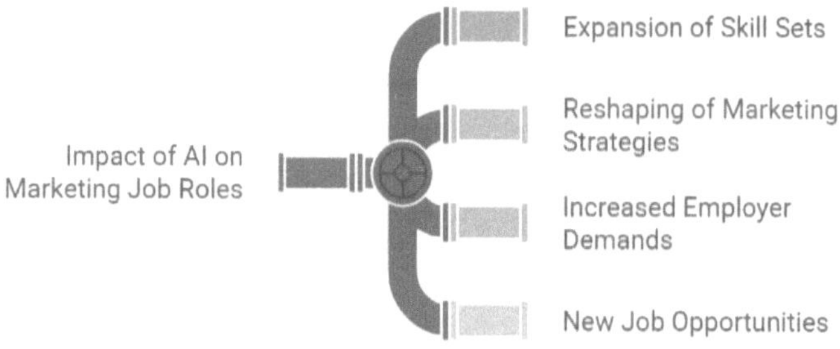

Increased Employer Demands

Demands from employers are changing as a result of the increasing use of AI in marketing. Having a good grasp of AI is quickly rising in demand. Businesses are seeking marketers with a unique combination of creative and analytical skills, able to understand and interpret data and AI algorithms. Now, employers place a premium on:

- "Hybrid talent": which combines artistic ability with technological proficiency
- Lifelong Learning: Being able to adjust to new strategies and tools enabled by AI

New Job Opportunities

Last but not least, AI opens up new doors in the marketing world. Machine learning engineers in advertising, AI marketing specialists, and countless more positions were unimaginable just a few years ago, but now they're commonplace thanks to the proliferation of AI. If you're qualified, the marketing and AI junction is a hotspot for profitable jobs, and the labor market is humming along.

We are entering an era driven by artificial intelligence, and marketers will need to adapt by learning new things, coming up with new tactics, meeting more demands, and taking advantage of new career prospects. Artificial intelligence (AI) isn't anything to be afraid of as a marketing professional; in fact, it's essential if you want to succeed in this new age.

Possible Challenges with AI in Marketing

Aspirations of marketers worldwide typically accompany forays into the realm of artificial intelligence (AI). Process simplification, marketing strategy optimization, and redefining of sales targets are common outcomes of making use of its extensive set of capabilities. Despite AI's many potential benefits, the technology is not without its share of challenges. Despite how appealing it may sound, using AI into marketing campaigns won't magically fix every issue. Instead, it presents a plethora of new challenges that businesses will need to carefully overcome.

Data Security and Privacy Concerns

Concerns about personal information and data security rank high among these issues. There are significant worries over the security of AI in handling consumer data in an age when personal information is worth more than gold dust. Because AI relies on massive amounts of user data to function, these algorithms store a plethora of personally identifiable information. There must be immediate implementation of stringent security measures to prevent breaches and theft caused by this data vulnerability. The necessity for legislation that strike a balance between the rights of individuals to privacy and the goals of AI is increasing in tandem with the globalization of markets. An instance of this is the recently enacted General Data Protection Regulation (GDPR) by the European Union. The most important thing for marketers to do is to be honest with their clients about how they use their personal data and to assure them that their privacy is safe.

Affordability and Implementation Barriers

One of the biggest problems that businesses encounter when trying to use AI in their marketing is the cost. The upfront expenses of developing AI systems can be enormous, but the long-term savings in labor and materials could be well worth it. Small and medium-sized organizations are often discouraged from using these technologies due to the substantial investments required in hardware, software, and specialist personnel. In addition, deep knowledge in data science and ML is necessary for effective AI deployment. The equation is further complicated by the shortage of such competent resources. Additionally, incorporating AI into preexisting marketing systems can be a complex and challenging process that requires meticulous preparation and faultless implementation.

Insufficient Understanding and Trust

The world of perception presents a less concrete but no less formidable obstacle for marketers utilizing AI. Many people find the complexities of AI to be confusing, if not completely bewildering. Many people are wary of putting their faith in AI systems for important marketing decisions because of this misunderstanding. Businesses should invest in educating their marketing staff and, by implication, their customers, about AI in order to gain their trust. More widespread use of AI can be achieved by openness regarding its strengths, weaknesses, and privacy protections.

Regulation Impact

From a legislative standpoint, there are further obstacles to AI in marketing. Companies' use of AI is directly affected by worldwide privacy legislation such as GDPR (General Data Protection Regulation). Consequently, it is critical to successfully traverse the complex terrain of regulatory mandates and ethical principles. It is becoming more difficult for organizations to keep up with the ever-changing regulatory landscape surrounding AI. Artificial intelligence (AI) opens up a world of possibilities for marketers, but it also brings its fair share of challenges. In order to succeed with AI-powered marketing, stakeholders must be informed about potential obstacles and actively plan to overcome them as technology keeps getting better and more integrated into our lives.

Conclusion

A world of revolutionary possibilities opens up as we look into the future of artificial intelligence in marketing. Businesses may improve their productivity, provide customers with more tailored experiences, and come up with more effective strategies by implementing intelligent systems. As we enter a new year, the world of global business is about to be transformed by the merging of artificial intelligence and marketing. Having said that, great power also brings great responsibility. A number of obstacles stand in the way of an AI-driven marketing landscape, including worries about data security, price, trust, and regulatory implications. Ethical and technological solutions must be prioritized as organizations deftly handle these concerns.

Rising Action:
Part I

AI Essentials Checklist[17]

With the support of Google AI, you can increase your company's success by attracting new customers, producing top-notch content, and making informed decisions. Are you prepared to succeed with artificial intelligence? Review the following checklist for ways to immediately supercharge your marketing using Google AI after you have established your marketing goals and connected them to your larger business ambitions.

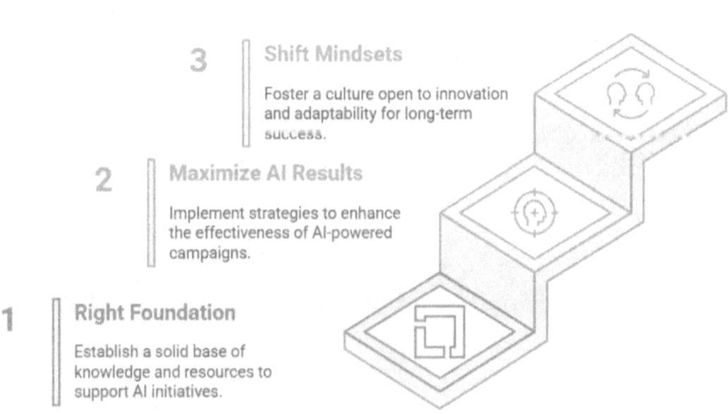

1. Get ready with the right foundation

   Optimize your return on investment (ROI) and business results with the help of Google AI by bolstering your measurement approach with high-quality consented data. The direct relationships you have with your consumers provide you with first-party data, which is highly useful.

   - To get the most important data, you should use the Google tag to set up robust site-wide tagging. Ads serving the UK and the EU should employ approval Mode to build a solid system for gathering and keeping users' approval.

- To make your conversion measurement more accurate, set up improved conversions.

- Based on your business goals, such as revenue, profit margins, or lifetime value, assign values to your conversions.

- Google Analytics 4 will help you understand your apps and websites better.

- To reconnect with your consumers across all of Google's platforms, try using Customer Match.

- Prioritize high-quality creative inputs, such as website content, and use our AI-powered creative tools to construct a variety of campaign materials.

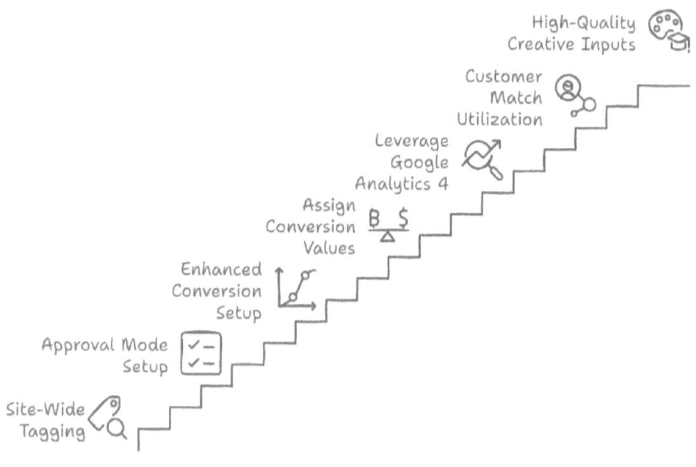

2. Take action to maximise results with AI-powered campaigns:

With campaigns driven by AI, you can optimize performance in real-time to maximize conversions and budget efficiency. Discover unmet needs and generate incremental revenue through innovative use of search, channels, and audiences.

- Turn on the feature that pairs ads: In order to increase conversions across all of Google, combine AI-powered search marketing with broad match with Performance Max campaigns.

- Invest in the conversions that matter most to your organization by using Smart Bidding across campaigns based on value.

- Use video campaigns to connect with your audience on YouTube, connected TV, and YouTube Shorts.

Maximizing AI-Powered Campaigns

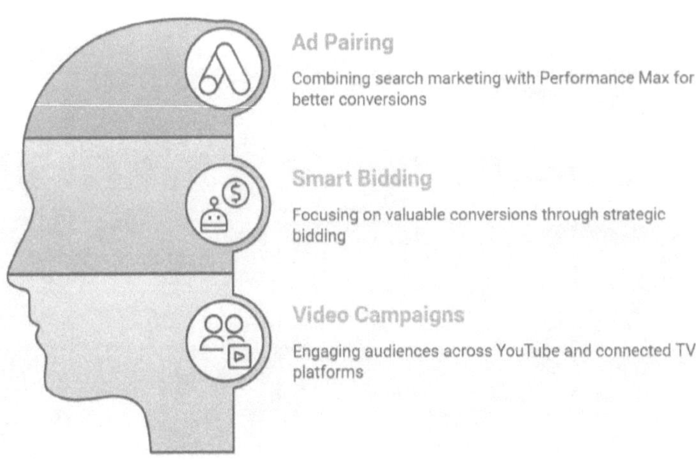

3. Shift mindsets to set your org up for success:

    Organizations can't get the most out of Google AI unless they take action to try new things, become more agile, and allocate resources to where they will have the greatest impact.

    - You have to get the upper management on board with reimagining marketing as an investment in growth rather than an expense. Establish clear alignment between marketing KPIs and business objectives.

    - Collaborate with your CFO to measure the marketing department's influence on critical financial indicators. The three pillars of experimentation—test, learn, and scale—must be established.

    - Eliminate data, budget, and channel silos to remain agile.

What is a Google Tag[18]?

A number of Google goods and services can be integrated into your website with the help of the Google tag (gtag. js). You can utilize a single Google tag throughout all of your website and connect it to many destinations, saving you the trouble of managing separate tags for each of your Google product accounts.

You may track how well your website and ads are doing by sending data from your site to related Google product destinations using the Google tag. Only Google Ads, Google Analytics 4, and Campaign Manager 360 allow users to view and configure the Google tag at this time. If you want more precise conversion measurements and access to stronger bids, enhanced conversions is the feature for you. By securely transmitting hashed first-party conversion data from your website to Google, it enhances your current conversion tags. Your first-party customer data, like email addresses, is securely encrypted before being sent to Google by utilizing a one-way hashing process known as SHA256. Enhanced conversions can be configured with the use of the Google tag, Google Tag Manager, or the Google Ads API.

How it works?

Customer`s names, email addresses, physical addresses, and phone numbers are examples of first-party customer data that may be collected when they make a purchase on your website. Your conversion tracking tags can collect this data, hash it, and then send it to Google so they can utilize it to improve your conversion measurement. The hashed data can be utilized in various ways to enhance your measurement, depending on the sort of enhanced conversions you choose to use.

Customer Success Stories

1. North Face:

   The North Face aimed to optimize the customer experience by understanding local tastes and needs in each market it operates in. That's why the company keeps tabs on the terms people use to find products online. The firm found out that its clients were searching for a new phrase, "midi parka, " by combining Google Tag Manager 360 with Google Analytics 360. In response to this realization, The North Face rebranded a product and saw a tripling in conversions and income.

2. Air France :

   After rolling out Consent Mode to all of their European markets, Air France saw a 9% increase in conversions. Thanks to Google's ability to model for conversion gaps when users don't consent to cookies, Consent Mode enabled sustainable measurement for Air France.

What is meant by Enhanced Conversions?

With conversion values, you can adjust your ad campaigns based on their actual impact on your business. More than just the overall number of conversions, you may understand the complete business value that Google Ads generated by assigning values to them. High-value conversions can also be located and targeted with more ease.

- You may monitor and improve your campaigns' return on investment (ROI) with the use of conversion values.

- To maximize your conversion value, such sales revenue or profit margins, while aiming to meet your target return on ad spend (ROAS), you can employ the Target (ROAS: Return on Ad Spend) bid strategy.

- If you don't have a set goal for your return on ad spend, you may still maximize your campaign's overall conversion value within your daily budget by using the Maximize conversion value bid strategy.

Additional advantages of conversion values are as follows:

Better insight: You may find out how much money your campaigns made from conversions in total. To measure the return on investment (ROI) of your campaigns, you can use the "Conversion value/cost" column. By analyzing this data, you can determine which campaigns, ad groups, and keywords yield a high or poor ROI, and then adjust your budget, targeting, and bids accordingly.

Smarter bidding: To achieve your performance goals across campaigns, ad groups, and keywords, automated bid strategies will automatically establish bids based on the conversion values you've put up.

- Aiming for a specific return on ad spend (ROAS) is possible with Target ROAS by setting bids to maximize conversion value, which can be defined as sales revenue or profit margins. To optimize bids for each auction and maximize conversion value, use the Maximize conversion value feature

Enhanced conversions for web:

- This is appropriate for marketers interested in monitoring website traffic and conversions.

- It makes it easier to track internet sales.

Whenever a user makes a purchase on your website, you can give them hashed first-party data. The information is subsequently utilized to associate your clients with the Google accounts that were active when they interacted with your ad.

Enhanced conversions for leads:

- Ads that want to monitor conversions from website leads that go away from the web (by phone or email, for instance) should find this information useful.

- It measures offline purchases made by leads or visitors to a website more accurately.

- It permit offline lead measurement using hashed, first-party user-provided data from online lead forms.

The hashed information you supply when you upload leads is what Google uses to link your ad campaign.

Set up conversion value measurement

You need to set up conversion value measurement before you can utilize it for insights or Smart Bidding.

Measure different values for each conversion:

Setting it up can be more of a hassle, but the results are more accurate representations of the transaction amounts. If the conversion value of each of your sales is different, you might want to consider using transaction-specific conversion values for your firm.

Measure the same value for each conversion:

Although it's less complicated to set up, it might not accurately reflect the varying values of each transaction. If you need to approximately differentiate between many conversion actions, using identical conversion values could be a good choice.

What is meant by Smart Bidding?

With the help of Smart Bidding, which uses billions of permutations of signals to personalize your bids for each ad auction, you may achieve your marketing objectives. It makes superior real-time bids with the help of Google AI. Here we'll go over the benefits of measuring conversion values and how to use a value-based Smart Bidding approach to improve the performance of your Search ads.

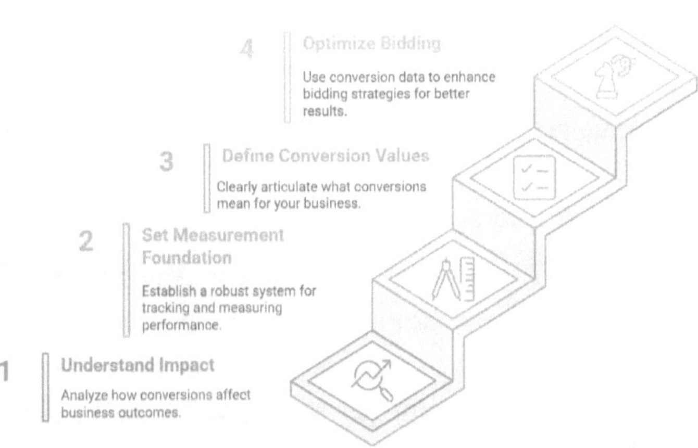

To maximize the effectiveness of your advertising initiatives, make sure to adhere to following recommended practices:

1. Understand business impact through conversion values: Assigning values to conversions improves the measurement and optimization of your ad campaign's actual impact.

   - You can't just focus on conversion rates when calculating the worth of Google Ads for your company.

- Optimize your advertising approach by identifying high-value conversions.

- The "Conversion value/cost" column is a great tool for monitoring ROI. It is important to find out where your budget and goals need tweaking by using this data.

2. Set up a measurement foundation: Establish a firm groundwork for efficiently constructing and measuring data. When done in accordance with your company goals, this will allow you to fully utilize your first-party (1P) data. Here's how it works:

   - The proper capture of conversion actions, including online purchases or lead form submissions, depends on your tagging configuration. Verify that your Google tag or Google Tag Manager is configured correctly. Because of this, you can rest assured that Google's AI-powered products are using accurate and thorough IP data.

   - Google Ads Data Manager allows you to connect to additional IP data sources, so you can access your data no matter where it resides. Customer relationship management systems, marketing technologies, customer data platforms, and cloud storage are all part of this category.

   - Make use of improved conversions to ensure long-lasting and precise measurement.

   - To strengthen your current conversion tags, enable enhanced conversions for the web.

   - Take advantage of improved lead conversions to share statistics about offline conversions.

- Make use of attribution models that are powered by data to ensure a more precise allocation of value throughout your customers' journey. The real effect of each touchpoint on conversions can then be better understood.

- Your bid optimization goal should be a specific stage of your lead-to-sale funnel; ideally, it should have a short conversion latency and generate at least 15 conversions each month.

- Make sure you have the most current data for optimization by tracking and uploading conversions often, preferably daily.

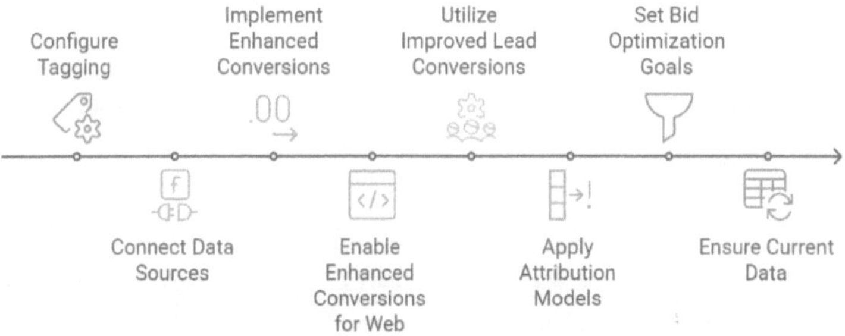

3. Define your conversion values: Select the values that best correspond with your business objectives and internal resources to initiate the sharing of conversion value through your measurement setup:

   - Static values: Select to allocate a singular value for each conversion action. This system, although simpler to implement, may not adequately reflect the diverse values of each transaction. Utilizing consistent conversion values can aid in distinguishing various conversion procedures. It is essential to measure a minimum of two distinct values throughout at least two different actions, ensuring that neither value is zero.

- Dynamic values: Assess the distinct valuation of each conversion for your enterprise. This method offers a more precise depiction of transaction values. Transaction-specific conversion values are optimal when each sale possesses a distinct value for your enterprise.

4. Optimize bidding with conversion values: Employ value-based Smart Bidding methods utilizing the established conversion values.

- Utilize Maximize Conversion Value with a target Return on Ad Spend (ROAS) to optimize bids for maximizing conversion value, including sales revenue or profit margins, while striving to meet your specified ROAS objective.

- Utilize Maximize Conversion Value without a target, wherein bids for each auction are tailored to enhance conversion value within a predetermined budget.

5. Additional Tricks:

- Use conversion value rules: Apply multiplication factors to conversion values for specific customer types, devices, or locations to optimize for higher value actions.

- Utilize new customer acquisition goals: Efficiently acquire new customers through your Google Ads campaigns by setting up goals tailored to new customer acquisition.

- Evaluate performance with bid strategy reports: Utilize the bid strategy report to assess performance over time and gain insights into how well your bidding strategies align with your conversion value objectives.

Customer Success Story: BAUR

For their most recent Google Ads campaign, German e-commerce platform BAUR used Google Analytics. They saw a 56% uptick in sales after targeting an audience of probable buyers. According to BAUR's calculations, employing these predictive audiences in Google Ads was the only way to reach 70% of these clients.

About Customer Match:

By utilizing Customer Match, you can leverage both online and offline first-party data to expand your customer reach and engagement across various Google properties, such as Search, the Shopping tab, Gmail, YouTube, and Display.

By analyzing your consumer data, Google AI is able to fine-tune its audience and bidding techniques, resulting in more targeted, high-performing ads for your best consumers. For instance, a 5.3% increase in conversions was observed when advertisers included Customer Match list signals in their advertisements. Customer Match can assist you in strengthening and expanding your relationships with customers in various ways including:

- It can upsell your current clients on additional products or services they might be interested in.

- It can communicate with your current clientele and offer them exclusive deals.

- It can reengage inactive clients.

- It can seek out new clients who are comparable to your most significant clients.

As we move towards a cookieless world, Customer Match lists will enable you to continue reaching your most valuable customers and will be an important tool to help you manage your audiences, in addition to tag-based website visitors.

Customer Match lists, along with tag-based website visits, will be an important tool for audience management as we progress towards a cookieless world. They will allow you to continue reaching your most valuable customers.

Google Ads will keep letting advertisers use their own data (including custom and expanded audiences) on Google owned and operated (O&O) properties through existing Customer Match products, even after third-party cookies are deprecated. This is because there will be no changes to the current policies regarding advertiser data.

To enhance your client engagement with client Match, adhere to following best practices:

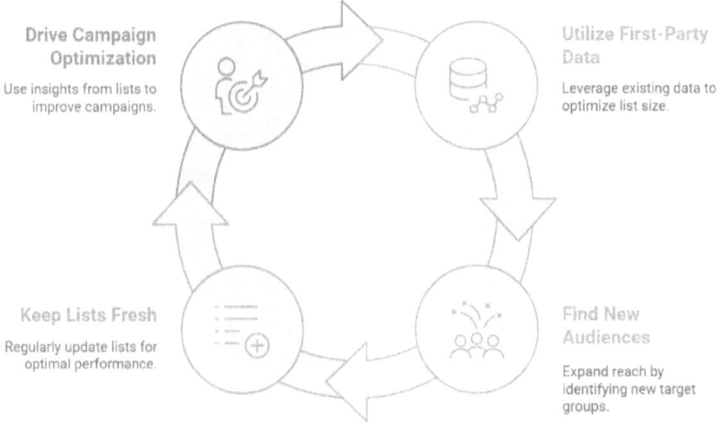

- **Utilize your current first-party data to optimize list size.**

  - Upload all available types of first-party data from your customers—like email address, mobile device, phone number, and physical address—in the right format to create the largest possible audience list size.

  - To generate the biggest audience list size possible, upload all first-party data from your clients in the appropriate format, including their email address, phone number, mobile device, and physical address. Employing a validated Customer Match upload partner optimizes the time-consuming task of uploading your customer list. It also enables the inclusion of further information, which can significantly enhance match rates and expand list size. Upon uploading client information to Google, the data is hashed—converted into encrypted codes—and subsequently matched with the codes of Google accounts. Upon completion of the matching process, the codes are promptly removed. Regardless of the existence of a match, Google neither retains this data nor use it for any other Google product.

- Utilize match rate as a criterion to identify any data formatting discrepancies: The match rate indicates the proportion of your upload that successfully connects to Google's logged-in users, hence revealing the usability of your list. Do not worry if your match rate is not 100%; it is typical to encounter unmatched consumer information. Utilize it as a benchmark for assessing the viability and proper formatting of your data. The match rates for the majority of advertising range from 29% to 62%. To enhance your match rate, ensure that your list is formatted and encrypted correctly.

- Incorporate many sources of client information within a single row of your data file: This guarantees the highest precision in match rate inside Google Ads. For instance, when you possess a phone number and an email address from the same client, position them in the same row adjacent to one another (as illustrated in row 2 and row 5).

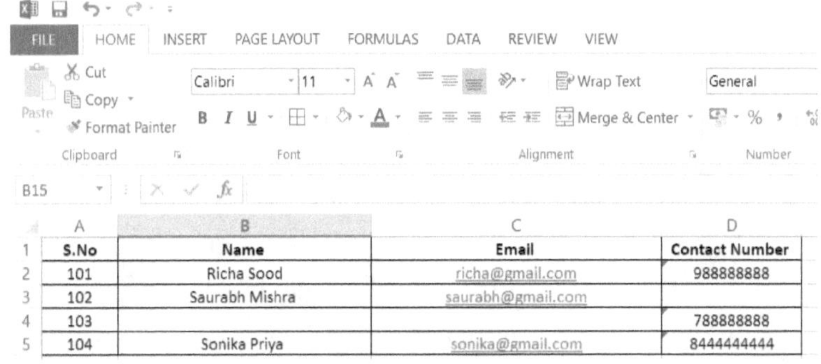

S.No	Name	Email	Contact Number
101	Richa Sood	richa@gmail.com	988888888
102	Saurabh Mishra	saurabh@gmail.com	
103			788888888
104	Sonika Priya	sonika@gmail.com	8444444444

Optimizing First-Party Data for Audience Expansion

1 — Data Upload
Uploading data in the correct format to expand audience reach

2 — Format Verification
Ensuring data is in the appropriate format for use

3 — Match Rate Assessment
Evaluating match rates to identify formatting issues

4 — Data Integration
Combining multiple data sources into a single row

- **Find new audiences:**

  - Activate the new customer acquisition objective in Google Ads: This AI-driven strategy utilizes your current customer databases to discover and engage potential new clients. Select your customer lists and establish your customer acquisition value, and your campaign will optimize for new consumers.

  - Generate Customer Match lists from leads via lead form audiences: Lead form audiences are automatically populated with people who have submitted information to your lead form assets. Segments can be created, managed, and utilized based on your form replies.

- **Keep lists fresh for optimal performance:**

  - Regularly refresh Customer Match lists: Failure to update your lists results in obsolescence, constraining the data available to Google for identifying your pertinent audience and enhancing campaign optimization. Here are the methods to update your lists:

    - When choosing manual uploads in Google Ads, it is advisable to establish a calendar reminder to update lists at the same day and time each week.

    - If you choose API-based uploads, the optimal practice is to automate your upload process to append to lists at least once daily.

    - If you choose to utilize a Customer Match upload partner, the optimal practice is to collaborate with an upload partner to facilitate the frequent refresh of lists.

    - When selecting a third-party automated solution, such as Zapier, the optimal approach is to configure a "Zap" that will automatically update lists in real time.

    - If you choose Conversion-based customer lists, the recommended procedure is to go Account Settings and select the checkbox labeled "Turn on conversion-based lists. "

- Utilize advanced conversions with Customer Match to automatically create customer lists aligned with your objectives: By utilizing enhanced conversions and activating conversion-based client lists, customer segments tailored to your organization will be automatically created according to your conversion objectives and updated in real-time. This indicates that customer lists will remain current without necessitating any work on your part.

- **Use your lists to drive campaign optimization**

  - Utilize your Customer Match lists in conjunction with AI-driven Smart Bidding and refined targeting to enhance performance: Smart Bidding and improved targeting utilize signals from your Customer Match lists to improve campaign performance in alignment with business objectives, such as conversions.

Case in Example: ImmoScout24

ImmoScout24, a prominent real estate platform in Germany, sought to enhance their audience strategy and optimize campaign success through the utilization of first-party consumer data. Following the enhancement of their tagging configuration, the upload of customer data, and the implementation of Customer Match across all Google Ads accounts, they experienced a 52% increase in conversion rate and a 15% reduction in cost-per-acquisition.

About Creative Performance

Creative assets are more vital to performance. Research indicates that your creative contributes to 49% of the overall sales impact of advertising. Consumers anticipate highly relevant, tailored experiences from the brands they interact with at every touchpoint. AI-driven solutions can provide innovative variations with the speed, quality, and volume necessary to engage your consumers effectively.

Adhere to the following best practices to optimize your creativity:

1. **Provide quality and quantity:**

   Provide Google with diverse inputs to ascertain effective outcomes. Ensure the dissemination of a variety of on-brand creative materials, including a robust website, picture assets, and your firm logo.

   - Create a website featuring a variety of pertinent landing pages that serve as the definitive reference for your business. Search and Performance Max by Google Ads may extract information, including your business logo and name, as well as visuals to create new creative assets. The accuracy, specificity, and recency of the input from your website are crucial, as obsolete information can jeopardize your campaign.

   - Strive for both quality and quantity: Incorporate a variety of headlines and descriptions to enable Google AI to evaluate diverse combinations and identify the most effective options. This will guarantee that every ad group in your Search campaign contains at least one responsive search ad with 'Good' or 'Excellent' Ad Strength.

- Incorporate picture assets into your Search advertising to visually present your products, or activate dynamic image assets to allow Google AI to autonomously select the most pertinent photos from your landing pages and attach them to your advertisements.

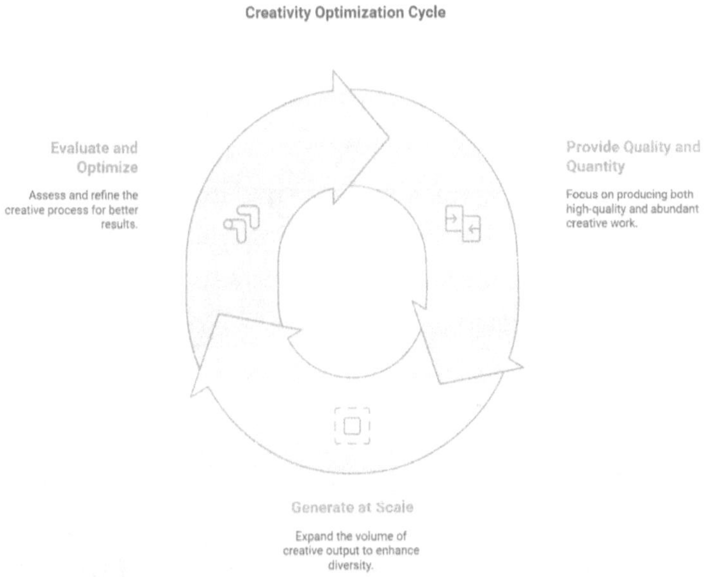

2. Generate at scale:

- Google AI assists in the efficient and scalable development of superior assets. You can enhance the creative process by collaborating with Google AI-driven solutions.

Generate new:

- For more targeted advertising, turn on automatically generated assets in your Search and Performance Max in Google Ads campaigns. Automatically generated materials will consistently provide new headlines and descriptions that are more precisely aligned with customers' specific context and intent, while remaining faithful to your brand and offers.

- You should utilize the novel asset generation and generative AI functionalities in Performance Max. It is possible to create novel headlines, descriptions, and lifestyle photographs pertinent and distinctive to your brand directly within the Google Ads UI.

- Use the conversational experience in Google Ads to create a Search campaign—complete with AI-generated suggestions for headlines, images, keywords, and more—through chat.

Augment existing assets:

- Make a video in at least three different orientations using the video maker: vertically, horizontally, and squarely using the help of Google AI, you can intelligently convert your movies to different aspect ratios, and using Trim Video, you can make Bumpers out of lengthier films.

- Use Product Studio in Merchant Center Next to improve the images of your products that you already have. You can easily edit your product photos to make them relevant for different types of customers, offers, and ad formats.

3. Evaluate & Optimize:

Comprehend your performance, refine your approach, and intensify efforts on successful strategies. By acquiring the appropriate insights, one can get a comprehensive grasp of which creative elements resonate with the audience.

- Disseminate Knowledge: Disseminate knowledge regarding high-performing content and audience assets to creative teams to initiate effectively. Your creative teams and Google AI will utilize these to generate new assets for testing.

- Integrate your first-party data with Google AI: Integrate your first-party data with Google AI to generate enhanced creative ideas and elevate the quality of your assets, potentially resulting in improved performance. Your creative may yield superior results if customized to the specific stage of the sales funnel relevant to your buyer or the geographical region in which they encounter your advertisement.

- Monitor Ad Strength: Ad Strength offers anticipatory feedback that aids in assessing the adherence of an advertisement to best practices for optimal performance and identifies actionable steps for enhancement.

- Utilize the Insights page: Utilize the Insights page to analyze emerging performance trends and conduct trials on novel concepts. This will enable your brand to consistently present itself optimally in both evergreen and seasonal creative contexts.

Customer Success Story: Armani Beauty

Armani Beauty, a brand within L'Oréal's portfolio, sought methods to enhance on-site conversions through pertinent and captivating Search advertisements. To engage a broader audience with pertinent advertisements, the team incorporated responsive search ads into each ad group of its unbranded campaigns, ensuring they achieved "Good" or "Excellent" Ad Strength. They incorporated assets, such as sitelinks and photos, inside each ad group to facilitate quicker action from potential customers. Consequently, Armani experienced a 61% rise in click-through rate and an 11% increase in on-site transactions.

Mobile Advertising Assessment Study Guide[18]

Importance of Mobile Advertising:

It is essential for business website to function effectively on mobile devices; therefore, if you have not yet prioritized making your website mobile-friendly, it is imperative to do so now. Here are few reasons why your mobile presence is essential to your business:

- Mobile-optimized websites rank higher in search results.

- Mobile queries constitute over fifty percent of searches on Google. com.

- A significant portion of traffic for numerous marketers originates from mobile phone users.

- If your website is not optimized for mobile, visitors are five times more likely to exit.

Is your website mobile-friendly?

Envision yourself as a prospective client accessing your website on your mobile device. What is the loading speed of your website? How simple is it to locate the desired information? Mobile visitors to your website anticipate immediate responses. They will seek to rapidly acquire knowledge about your enterprise and determine their level of interest. Their experience on your website will significantly impact their perception of your organization and the probability of their conversion into customers. Optimizing your website for mobile entails prioritizing straightforward, intuitive navigation that facilitates user access to desired content.

Let us examine the components that contribute to a good mobile website:

- **Is your website optimized for rapid loading times?** Approximately fifty percent of all visitors will abandon a mobile website if the pages fail to load within three seconds. Reduce loading time (the duration required for a webpage to display on your screen) to provide swift and effortless navigation for visitors on your website.

- **Is navigation straightforward?** On a little display, individuals may struggle to locate their desired content. The greater the effort required by visitors to locate information, the higher the likelihood of their frustration and subsequent departure. Facilitate visitor navigation by streamlining your site menu and ensuring all content is readily visible without necessitating magnification for readability.

- **Is it simple to initiate action?** Your mobile website must facilitate swift and effortless execution of typical operations for users, including contacting you, searching for a product, or completing a transaction. Strive to reduce the number of steps required to finalize a form or transaction.

You can see how your site scores on mobile speed, and get quick fixes to improve it on **https://pagespeed. web. dev/**

Optimizing website for specific business goal:

The efficacy of your mobile website, notwithstanding its rapid loading and user-friendly navigation, hinges on its ability to encourage business transactions.

To optimize your website for mobile, consider the primary business objective that holds the greatest significance for you. What actions do you like your clients to undertake on your website? Purchase a particular item? Complete a contact form? When you clearly define the desired activity for users on your website, they are more inclined to undertake that action.

Based on your marketing objective, you should concentrate on design enhancements that motivate visitors to perform your intended action. Below are few recommendations tailored to certain objectives:

- *To increase online sales*

  - **Enhance site navigation efficiency:** Optimize your site menu to ensure all elements are accessible without the need for zooming in to read.

  - **Ensure information is accessible**: Facilitate consumer exploration before to purchase by utilizing expanding product graphics.

  - **Assist individuals in completing their purchases:** Position all instructions or "Buy now" buttons prominently at the forefront. Utilize current account information to minimize data entry for your clients, if feasible.

  - **Enable individuals to continue from a desktop**: Facilitate the return of individuals to their shopping basket on desktop computers, enabling them to complete their transactions.

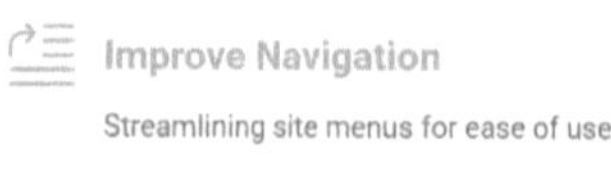

- To get more phone calls:

  - **Utilize click-to-call buttons or hyperlinks:** Refrain from requiring individuals to memorize your number or to magnify it for clarity.

  - **Streamline your menu selections:** Ensure it is evident that telephone calls are the most effective means of contacting your organization. Display a clickable telephone number or button on each page of your website.

  - **Avoid diversions:** Minimize advertisements and other distractions to allow individuals to concentrate on contacting you by phone.

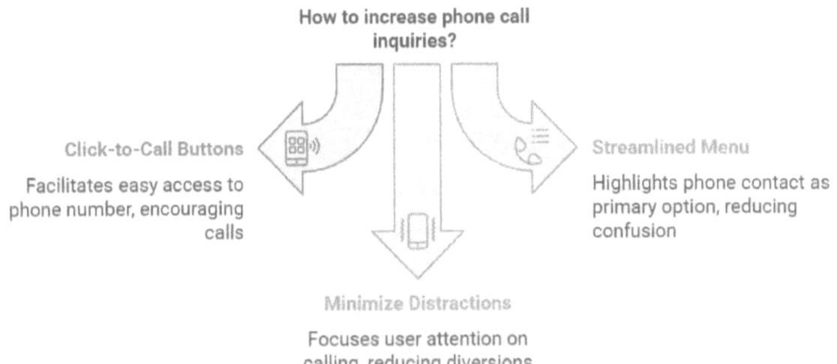

- *To drive more online leads*

  - **Streamline your forms:** Ensure that individuals can readily access your forms, and that data entry is streamlined and convenient for thumb use.

  - **Restrict scrolling and zooming:** Your form must occupy only the area allowed on a mobile display. The actions of scrolling and zooming complicate the process for individuals, increasing the likelihood of errors during information entry.

  - **Select your data fields judiciously:** Ensure that the information requested in your form is readily accessible and easily verifiable. Employ validation to display errors for unfilled fields.

Optimizing Forms for Online Leads

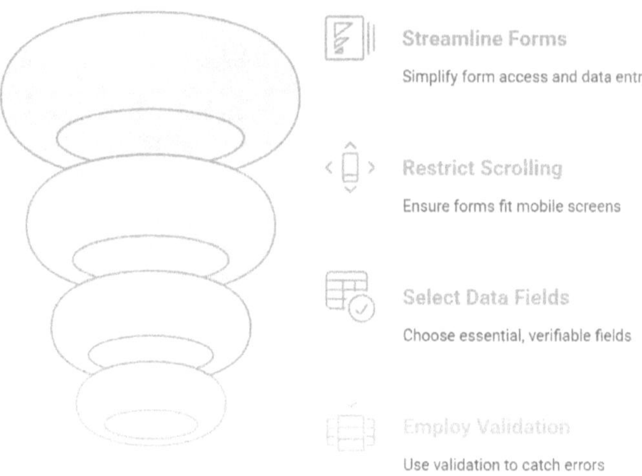

- *To encourage store visits:*

  - **Encourage visits mostly:** Emphasize that visiting your physical business is the optimal choice for customers. Display a map, location button, or icon that directly links to your actual address and business hours on every page of the website.

  - **Limit material:** Optimize your website's navigation to furnish sufficient information that persuades individuals to visit your store.

  - **Avoid diversions:** Promotions can effectively persuade individuals to patronize your store; however, they should not complicate navigation.

- *To disseminate information and awareness*

  - **Enhance navigation efficiency:** Implement a straightforward menu and utilize larger font to assist individuals in conducting research prior to making a purchase commitment. Due to the reduced size of mobile screens, streamline your menu selections to prevent overwhelming users.

  - **Maintain uniformity between devices:** The longer a customer delays their purchase decision, the more probable it is that they will conduct research across various devices (laptop, tablet, phone) prior to finalizing the deal. Regardless of the device in use, assist them in resuming their previous activity by preserving their selections.

  - **Include a hyperlink to the homepage:** Ensure that those who have reached an impasse in their research may easily navigate back to the homepage to initiate a new search.

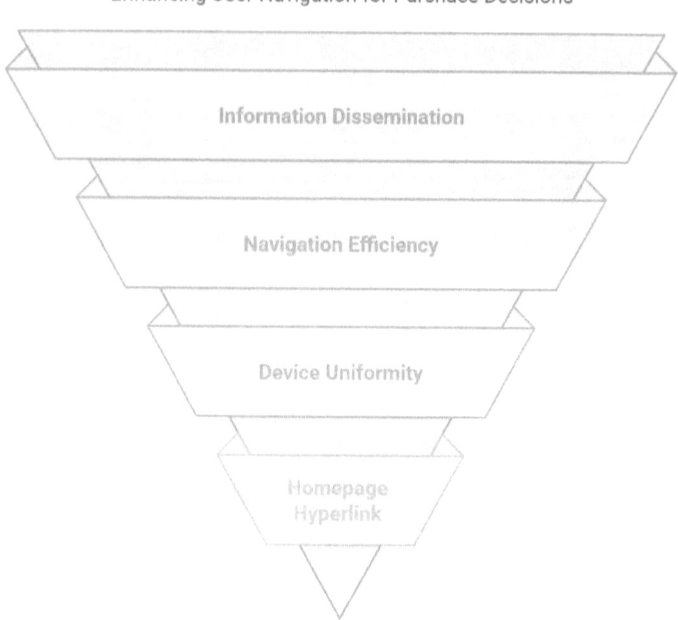

Optimize your ads for mobile:

1. Use the right ad assets for mobile

Ad assets enable the display of supplementary business information alongside your advertisement, such as an address, telephone number, or connections to particular pages on your website. These materials enhance the visibility and attractiveness of your advertisements for mobile users. Utilizing ad assets incurs no expense; nonetheless, standard charges apply for clicks on your advertisement.

Some of the advertising assets that can enhance mobile ad performance are :

- Add sitelink assets to drive online sales:

- Add location assets to drive store visits

- Add call assets to drive phone calls

2. **Follow best practices for writing effective mobile ads:**

To engage potential customers on mobile devices, your advertisements must be pertinent, persuasive, and informative. The key strategies that can be adopted for crafting an effective mobile advertisement are as follows:

- **Capture interest with engaging headlines:** The headline is the initial element that individuals observe. The clickable and most conspicuous element of your mobile advertisement should be prioritized for relevance and appeal. Incorporate your keywords to ensure that individuals immediately recognize the relevance of your advertisement to their search.

- **Employ a compelling call-to-action:** An emphatic and lucid call-to-action informs mobile visitors of what to anticipate and motivates them to undertake the desired action. Utilize potent verbs such as Purchase, Contact Today, Request, Enroll, or Obtain a Quote. Selecting an appropriate action phrase can save unnecessary expenditure on clicks that are unlikely to generate revenue for you.

- **Optimize your descriptive text:** Emphasize the distinctive qualities of your firm and the reasons it fulfills customer needs. Highlight your principal selling attributes (service, dependability, extensive variety, unique items, specific pricing or promotions, etc.) that distinguish you from competitors.

- **Rotate several ad variations:** When many ads exist inside an ad group, Google Ads will, by default, prioritize the display of those that perform better. It is advisable that marketers create 2 to 4 distinct advertisements, each featuring separate headlines or descriptive text.

3. Make sure your mobile landing page matches your ad

The mobile landing page significantly influences the conversion of clicks into buyers. When an individual clicks on your advertisement, they anticipate arriving at a website that is pertinent to the content of the ad they viewed. If users do not promptly discover what they anticipate, they are more inclined to exit your site.

Select a mobile landing page that reflects the call-to-action in your advertisement and offers a straightforward method to execute that action, such as acquiring a particular product or completing a form. All promotions or special offers advertised must be prominently displayed on your landing page.

The link between your mobile advertisement and landing page serves as the conduit for a prospective customer to engage in the desired action. A more robust correlation between your advertisement and landing page enhances your likelihood of achieving favorable outcomes.

Best practices guide: Setting up your App campaigns

It is advisable to share your goals and App campaigns so that they can use the power of Google AI to build, optimize, and match your ads with the right people for your business. With Google`s AI technology, App campaigns are able to analyze hundreds of millions of signal combinations and test different creative assets and channel combinations to serve the best-performing ads. Some of the key best practices to setting up a successful App campaign are:

1. **Define your goals to optimize your campaign**

   Articulate your objectives—be it augmenting installations, facilitating particular in-app activities, or encouraging people to pre-register for your application prior to its release. App campaigns will subsequently enhance your campaign bidding and targeting to achieve those aims. Examples of potential goals include:

- **Build a user base** :Develop an application campaign that prioritizes "Install volume" and aims at "All users" to maximize installations within a certain cost-per-install (CPI).

  - Establish a target Cost Per Install (CPI) predicated on the average value of a new user.

  - Establish a daily campaign budget for Google Ads that is a minimum of 50 times your desired Cost Per Install (CPI) to ensure sufficient data collection without exceeding your budget.

- **Engage users who complete in-app actions:** After identifying the most important in-app action for your business, establish an App campaign that optimizes for "In-app actions. "

  - Provide Google Ads with sufficient data to recognize new users who are inclined to perform an in-app activity. Select an in-app activity that is executed by a minimum of 10 distinct users daily inside the campaign.

  - Establish a target CPA predicated on the average value of a user that does the action.

  - Establish a daily campaign budget for Google Ads that is a minimum of ten times your goal CPA to ensure sufficient data collection.

- **Drive pre-registration sign ups for your app before it launches**

  - This campaign type employs the Target CPA bidding method to maximize conversions specifically for pre-registrations. By establishing your bid, you indicate to Google Ads the typical expenditure you wish to incur for each pre-registration of your app. The designated bid is target cost-per-pre-registration, which is automatically established at the initial pre-registration for your app.

2. **Upload diverse creative to generate the best-performing ads**

Supply a varied assortment of textual content along with high-caliber video and image resources. This allows App campaigns to autonomously produce original content that is optimized for maximum reach and performance across several platforms. Each ad group may have a maximum of 10 text assets, 20 picture assets, and 20 video assets, along with 20 HTML5/playable assets for mobile game advertisers. Consider the following innovative best practices:

- Compose independent sentences of varying lengths, as distinct advertising positions impose varied text limitations. Ensure that phrases emphasize unique selling propositions and incorporate conversational language with explicit calls to action.

- Image assets must occupy the entire advertisement frame with little blank space, exhibiting great pixel density and limited text overlay. Refrain from overlaying logos and calls-to-action.

- Video: Incorporate captivating videos with durations ranging from 10 to 30 seconds. Incorporate films in various aspect ratios, such as portrait, landscape, and square, to enhance eligibility across many advertising channels and accommodate the diverse orientations in which individuals utilize their devices.

Utilize Google's Ad strength meter to assess if your App campaign assets possess adequate diversity to optimize performance. Additionally, consistently evaluate your asset performance according to the ratings in your asset report and substitute underperforming assets with new ones.

3. **Set up deep links for more seamless web-to-app user experiences**

Consumers appreciate brands that provide a seamless web-to-app experience, facilitating easier interaction, which in turn enhances campaign performance for the brands. For customers who have your app loaded, you can provide this enhanced experience by utilizing deep links. Deep links guide people from your mobile web advertisement to the pertinent in-app information, facilitating actions such as completing a purchase or enrolling in a loyalty program. Advertisers utilizing deep linking experience, on average, more than a twofold increase in conversion rates.

Establishing this necessitates technological execution. To streamline these procedures, utilize Web to App Connect, a comprehensive platform offering guided instructions to assist marketing and development teams in efficiently establishing deep connections, along with conversion tracking and bidding mechanisms to guarantee the maximization of your campaign's worth.

4. **Adopt privacy-centric solutions for better campaign measurement**

User expectations about privacy are increasing, and evolving platform standards have complicated measurement. To adjust to these changes and achieve enduring outcomes, it is essential to adopt measurement best practices and privacy-focused solutions, including the following:

- Establish conversion monitoring to accurately assess the effectiveness of your App efforts in generating app installs and significant in-app activities for your business.

- Utilize Google Analytics 4 to get robust measurement functionalities that enhance your comprehension of engagement on your website and application, while optimizing your campaign efficacy. If you are currently utilizing a Google-approved App Attribution Partner for conversion monitoring, you may employ Google Analytics 4 as an auxiliary measuring tool.

- Comprehend the function of Google's conversion modeling in delivering an exhaustive assessment of your App campaign efficacy.

- Assess the feasibility of integrating your app into the SKAdNetwork measuring system for your iOS App campaigns. Additionally, contemplate the integration of the ATT prompt and on-device conversion measurement to enhance your recorded conversions.

Strategies for Optimizing and Measuring App Campaign Success

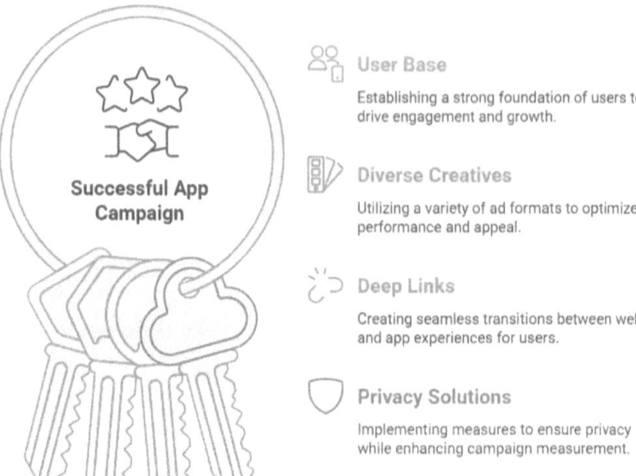

User Base

Establishing a strong foundation of users to drive engagement and growth.

Diverse Creatives

Utilizing a variety of ad formats to optimize performance and appeal.

Deep Links

Creating seamless transitions between web and app experiences for users.

Privacy Solutions

Implementing measures to ensure privacy while enhancing campaign measurement.

About Deep Links

Deep links guide mobile device users to pertinent pages within your application instead of your website. Users engage with advertisements and are redirected to your application sites. Deep links can be utilized in several Google Ads products, including App campaigns for engagement, App dynamic remarketing, and Search, Shopping, and Display campaigns.

Benefits:

- Enhanced security: App Links and Universal Links ensure that no other application can utilize your links. Other companies are unable to assert ownership of your link, thus preventing them from directing traffic to their own application, unlike what is achievable with bespoke schemes.

- Relevant page results: You can guide consumers and prospective customers to pertinent pages within your application, instead of browser or mobile web pages. App Links and Universal Links utilize the identical URL as your web links; therefore, if your app fails to open, users will be redirected to the mobile site landing page instead of encountering an error page.

- Fluid user experience: Enhanced integration for your application users elevates user experience, boosts conversions, and fosters customer loyalty.

Developer support required for deep linking:

Deep connections are not automatically configured upon app creation and function differently on iOS and Android platforms.

Your app development team must modify the application, and upon implementing App Links (Android) or Universal Links (iOS), a Digital Asset Link JSON file should be added to your website to redirect people to the app after it is installed. Implementing App Links or Universal Links will not alter the web URLs. This will enable web advertising such as Search, Shopping, and Display advertisements to route customers to installed applications.

Web to App Connect:

Deep linking and app conversion monitoring can be established with the Web to App Connect tool in Google Ads. Upon completing the setup for both, you can deliver a cohesive web-to-app experience for your clients, resulting in an average of twice the conversion rates for ad clicks directed to your app in comparison to your mobile website. This enhanced experience enables your clients to more effortlessly accomplish their desired actions, whether it be purchasing, registering, or adding products to their basket. Additionally, with the Web to App Connect interface, you can monitor in-app conversion behaviors and receive tips for enhancing your campaign. To initiate Web to App Connect, adhere to the three procedures outlined below:

1. Click the **Tools** icon ✂. in your respective Google Ads account.

2. Select the Planning dropdown in the section menu.

3. Select the App Advertising Hub. This will direct you to the Web to App Connect portal.

About conversion tracking:

Conversion tracking is a complimentary tool that reveals the outcomes after a customer's engagement with your advertisements—whether they acquired a product, subscribed to your newsletter, contacted your business, or downloaded your application. When a customer executes an action deemed worthwhile, these activities are referred to as conversions.

Why use conversion tracking:

- Identify the most effective keywords, advertisements, ad groups, and campaigns for generating value customer engagement.

- Comprehend your return on investment (ROI) to make more informed selections regarding your advertising expenditure.

- Utilize Smart Bidding tactics (including Maximize Conversions, target CPA, and target ROAS) that autonomously enhance your campaigns in alignment with your company objectives.

- Determine the number of customers potentially engaging with your advertisements on one device or browser and subsequently converting on another. Conversion data across devices, browsers, and other metrics may be accessed in your "All conversions" reporting column.

- Conversion tracking commences with the establishment of a conversion action within your Google Ads account. A conversion action refers to a certain consumer activity that holds significance for your business. Conversion tracking can be utilized to monitor the subsequent types of actions:

- Website actions: Transactions, registrations, and additional activities performed by clients on your website.

- Phone calls: Direct calls from your advertisements, calls to a telephone number listed on your website, and clicks on a telephone number on your mobile site.

- App installations and in-app activities: Installations of your Android or iOS mobile applications, as well as purchases or other actions conducted within such applications.

- If you possess both a website and a mobile application, you can establish app conversion tracking with Web to App Connect. After utilizing the Web to App Connect interface to establish conversion tracking and deep linking, enabling direct links from your advertisements to your business application, you can deliver a seamless web-to-app experience for your customers, resulting in an average of twice the conversion rates for ad clicks that direct to your app in comparison to your mobile website.

Web to App Connect enables users to effortlessly execute their desired actions, such as making purchases, registering, or adding goods to their cart. Additionally, with the Web to App Connect interface, you can monitor in-app conversion behaviors and receive tips for enhancing your campaign.

The conversion tracking method varies slightly for each conversion source; nevertheless, all types, excluding offline conversions, generally fit into one of the following categories:

- You incorporate a Google tag or code snippet into the code of your website or mobile application. Upon a customer clicking your advertisement on Google Search or designated Google Display Network sites, or viewing your video advertisement, a transient cookie is installed on their computer or mobile device. Upon the completion of the specified action, our system identifies the cookie via the incorporated code snippet, thereby documenting a conversion.

- Certain types of conversion tracking may not necessitate a tag. To monitor phone calls from call assets or call-only advertisements, utilize a Google forwarding number to ascertain the origin of the call from your ads, as well as to record specifics such as call duration, start and end times, and caller area code. Furthermore, app downloads and in-app purchases from Google Play, together with local actions, will be automatically documented as conversions, eliminating the necessity for tracking code.

Upon establishing conversion tracking, you may get statistics regarding conversions for your campaigns, ad groups, advertisements, and keywords. Analyzing this data in your reports can enhance your comprehension of how your advertising contributes to achieving critical objectives for your firm.

Rising Action:
Part II

Scaling creative work using Google`s Demand Gen AI

An evolution of focus is occurring. Individuals possess a seemingly infinite array of options for shopping, communication, and entertainment online. For advertising to be distinctive, it must be pertinent and beneficial – indeed, this is more crucial than ever. Enterprises must be present on all platforms with innovative assets that engage the audience's attention. Until now, achieving this at scale has seemed unattainable — however, generative AI is altering that perception. This technology enhances our ability to fulfill clients' requirements and reveals new opportunities throughout the marketing process, ranging from innovative immersive advertising experiences to high-performing creative assets.

Scaling creative production in line with brand standards

Google have been enhancing the efficiency and speed of producing high-quality creative materials for advertisements across various marketing platforms. The diversity of creative assets is essential for effective advertisements, and generative AI in Performance Max has facilitated this for a greater number of advertisers. Advertisers who enhance their Performance Max Ad Strength to Excellent experience, on average, a 6% increase in conversions. Event Tickets Center was among the initial beta testers for asset generation in Performance Max, enabling the team to enhance creative production by fivefold with reduced time and effort. Nonetheless, performance is not the sole criterion for creativity. Assets must align with brand guidelines. Advertisers will soon be able to share their typeface and color requirements in Performance Max, along with providing useful visual reference points to create new asset variations.

Google is also implementing new picture editing functionalities, allowing advertisers to incorporate more items, expand backdrops, and crop images to suit any format, size, and orientation. Furthermore, retailers will have the ability to showcase their products via their Google Merchant Center feeds and utilize these editing functionalities. As advertisers investigate innovative concepts, Google AI will produce further recommendations displaying products in various situations and scenarios, enabling advertisers to choose their preferred assets for use across marketing channels.

Bringing creative to life with new immersive ad experiences

Despite high-quality image and language materials in advertisements, customers may struggle to feel assured in their online purchasing selections without physically experiencing the goods or trying it on. Google's research indicates that this form of confidence is essential for brands. Generative AI can assist firms in effectively communicating their offerings and instilling consumer confidence directly through advertisements. Advertisers will soon boost their Shopping advertising with immersive visuals, such as Virtual Try-On and produced 3D ads. Additionally, a new feature will allow customers to explore an ad further to view product videos, summaries, and related products offered by the advertiser.

Google is presently evaluating a novel advertising experience in Search to assist individuals in navigating intricate purchasing decisions. Assume friends are undertaking renovations and are seeking "short-term storage. " Engaging with an advertisement for a storage facility may result in an interactive experience wherein artificial intelligence assists in determining requirements. By providing details such as images of furniture and their budget, users might use Google AI to suggest appropriate storage unit dimensions and packaging materials, along with a link for purchase on the website.

Driving results through visual storytelling

In addition to visually immersive advertisements, there exist chances to engage customers across our most visually captivating platforms – YouTube, Discover, and Gmail. Last year, Google initiated Demand Generation initiatives capable of reaching up to 3 billion consumers monthly. These campaigns have enabled advertisers to enhance demand and conversions, and Google will shortly extend them to additional advertisers on Display & Video 360 and Search Ads 360. YouTube Shorts has over 2 billion monthly logged-in visitors who explore new preferences via short-form videos. They are launching new formats and capabilities to assist businesses in engaging with viewers, including vertical ad formats, action-driven ad stickers, and new animated image advertising automatically generated from photos in advertisers' accounts and Demand Gen product feeds.

Creating opportunities to help consumers along their information journey

Advertisements have consistently played a crucial role in consumers' informational experiences. During Google I/O, we announced the deployment of AI Overviews in Search to all users in the U.S. , with additional countries to follow shortly. AI Overviews will be displayed in search results when they provide assistance that exceeds the current capabilities of Search. AI Overviews are prompting individuals to explore a wider array of websites for assistance with intricate inquiries; also, the links shown in AI Overviews receive more hits compared to regular online listings for the same query. Research indicates that individuals utilizing AI Overviews engage in Search more frequently and exhibit greater satisfaction with their outcomes. When individuals click links from AI Overviews, these interactions are of superior quality, resulting in users being more inclined to spend extended periods on the site. As Google persists in testing and enhancing the Search experience, they are likely to maintain emphasis on directing valuable traffic to publications and creators. Initial testing indicates that individuals see the advertisements positioned above and below the AI-generated summary as beneficial. Shortly, Google is likely to commence testing Search and Shopping advertisements in AI Overviews for users in the United States. They will have the chance to be featured in the AI Overview in a section explicitly designated as "sponsored" when pertinent to both the inquiry and the content of the AI Overview. No action is required from advertisers: Ads from current Search, Performance Max, and Standard Shopping campaigns may be displayed within the AI Overview. Google is likely to solicit feedback from advertisers and the industry.

Improving results with a strong foundation of measurement

Although these updates benefit businesses, the efficacy of AI is contingent upon the quality of the information provided. To maximize the benefits of AI, enterprises require a robust assessment approach grounded in first-party data. Numerous enterprises possess data from various sources, including conversion metrics, email lists, and polls. Until now, obtaining a comprehensive overview has been exceedingly intricate, particularly for small enterprises. The team members of Google are simplifying the process for advertisers through the availability of Google Ads Data Manager to all users. This enables advertisers to consolidate first-party data sources in a single location for use, analysis, and activation—transforming a process that formerly required weeks or months into mere minutes.

Putting Google AI to work for businesses

Informed by Google's AI principles and customer insights, these recent AI advancements will enable marketers to expand their vision, foster greater creativity, and accelerate outcomes. Google AI is designed to assist rather than supplant. Human creativity, strategic acumen, and expertise will perpetually confer an advantage to marketers.

Enhance visual storytelling in Demand Gen with generative AI

Demand Generation campaigns were launched last year to assist advertisers in generating and converting new demand through visual storytelling on Google's most engaging and entertainment-centric platforms – YouTube, YouTube Shorts, Discover, and Gmail. Google is now equipping brands and agencies with enhanced capabilities to convey captivating and engaging narratives in a rapid, non-linear digital environment. Generative image tools in Demand Gen will be deployed to advertisers globally in English, with other languages anticipated later. Utilizing Google AI, these applications generate impressive, high-quality image assets in within a few steps based on your specified instructions. If a marketer possess existing photographs that yield favorable results, he/she can create analogous options using the new "Generate more like this" tool.

Multiply your creative impact in seconds

Generative image tools enable more efficient testing of innovative concepts, whether by experimenting with novel image kinds or creating original designs from the ground up. Your experience is essential for assisting Google AI in producing photographs customized to your business or client's requirements. For instance, if you possess an outdoor lifestyle firm specializing in camping equipment, employ suggestions such as "vividly colored tents aglow beneath the Aurora Borealis" to generate visuals that will attract consumers planning camping excursions to Iceland. Demand Gen will now enable you to input text prompts to create additional picture assets according to your preferences. You will retain complete authority to determine which proposed images will be incorporated into your ads. Google is dedicated to adhering to our principles for the responsible development of generative AI technology, emphasizing justice, privacy, and security. In addition to ensuring that advertising material complies with the established Google Ads regulations, Google AI implements supplementary technical procedures to guarantee that generative image tools in Google Ads generate original and distinctive content i. e Google AI will never produce two similar photographs. All images produced by Google Ads incorporate identification mechanisms, including an open-standard markup visible in tools like Google Image Search, and a SynthID, an imperceptible digital watermark resilient to image manipulations such as screenshots, filters, and compression.

Creative storytelling on YouTube and Google:

1. To maintain audience engagement and achieve outcomes, advertisers must diversify their creative strategy through multi-format advertisements. Indeed, those executing both video and picture advertisements within Demand Gen campaigns experienced a 6% increase in conversions per

dollar compared to those utilizing image-only advertisements. Here are other recommendations to assist you in developing effective creatives for Demand Generation campaigns:

1. **Provide Google AI with the right assets** — Adhere to the rule of three by include a minimum of three photos and videos in each aspect ratio (vertical, square, and landscape) to optimize reach across all accessible inventory. Prioritize assets that are inherently suited to each format. When producing YouTube Shorts, emphasize vertical videos that are relatable, honest, and resonate with your audience.

2. **Use high-quality, relevant visuals** — Utilize premium, high-resolution films and graphics to cultivate brand trust and motivate client engagement. Retailers can customize their advertisements using product feeds that align with customers' interests. You can submit aspirational brief words and photos to your Merchant Center streams to enhance consumer consideration. Advertisers experience, on average, a 33% increase in conversions at a comparable cost per action (CPA) by including product feeds into Demand Generation campaigns.

3. **Evaluate and optimize performance** — Implement a test-and-learn approach while refining creative materials for your specific audiences and objectives. Examine asset reports to facilitate informed decisions regarding creative optimization.

Optimizing Creative Content for AI

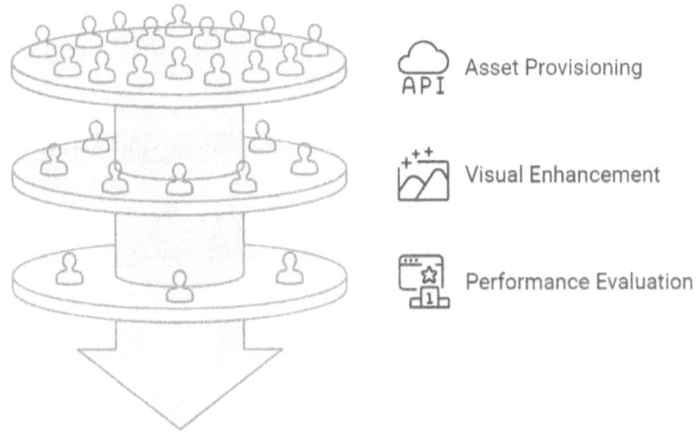

About the ABCDs of Effective Video Ads[18]

The four guiding concepts of successful YouTube video advertisements are connection, branding, direction, and attention.

1. Attention: Engage and maintain interest through a captivating narrative.

    *   Engage immediately: Accelerate to the core of the narrative and employ captivating pacing and concise framing to captivate the audience.

    *   Enhance the narrative with audio and subtitles: Augment your communication with auditory and textual elements. Eliminate competing elements.

    *   Ensure graphics are vibrant and high-contrast: Guarantee that visuals are optimized for all devices.

2. Branding: Brand frequently, abundantly, and with depth.

    *   Arrive promptly and remain present: Establish your brand or product from the outset and sustain that visibility.

    *   Augment with audio: Audio brand references improve the efficacy of onscreen brand images.

    *   Utilize all your branding resources: Employ a diverse array of branding elements to align with your message and objectives.

3. Connection: Facilitate emotional or cognitive engagement in individuals.

    *   Humanize the narrative: Incorporate individuals to enhance your product story and connect with your audience.

- Concentrate the message: Refrain from overloading your advertisement. Maintain message and terminology that is direct and uncomplicated.

- Engage: Utilize emotional triggers and narrative strategies, including humor, surprise, and suspense.

4. Direction: Request that they initiate action.

- Integrate a call to action (CTA): Be purposeful and incorporate a call to action to achieve a certain goal. Articulate your desired actions for the viewers.

- Enhance CTAs using audio: Augment your on-screen call to action with a voice-over to clarify the subsequent step.

Crafting Impactful YouTube Ads Through Key Strategies

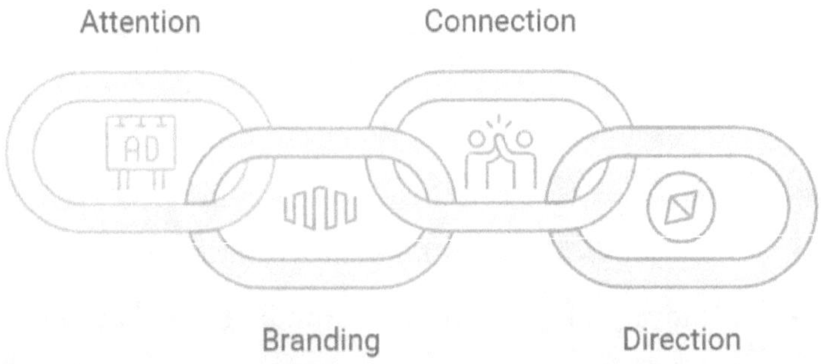

ABCDs by Marketing Objectives:

Effective video advertisements commence with the implementation of the Core ABCDs, however they can be refined to align with particular marketing objectives. Tailor your advertisements to accomplish your primary objectives using customized ABCD guidelines, whether your goal is to enhance awareness, stimulate contemplation, incite action, or a mix thereof.

Awareness: Get noticed:

- Attention: Enhance the audio to capture viewers' attention.

- Branding: Position your brand prominently

- Connection: Center the narrative on the individuals. Exhibit uniqueness while maintaining simplicity.

- Direction: Implement fundamental principles

Consideration: Show users how your product fits into their lives:

- Attention: Implement fundamental principles

- Branding: Make product the centre piece of attraction

- Connection: Demonstrate its functionality. Exhibit relatability

- Direction: Instill a sense of urgency

Action: Articulate a compelling call-to-action within the appropriate framework. :

- Attention: Implement fundamental principles

- Branding: Transform the product to become the advertisement.

- Connection: Be precise and concrete

- Direction: Articulate the request subsequent to establishing the context.

Full Funnel: Enhance efficacy by integrating all objectives:

- Attention: Capture attention with audio and concentrate on components that convey the message.

- Branding: Commence with a combination of branding components and conclude with the product.

- Connection: Forge a connection with your audience to bolster support for your goods.

- Direction: Incorporate calls to action throughout your advertisement, progressively adopting a more direct approach.

If you're a retailer, you can use product feeds to tailor your ads based on customers' interest. Upload aspirational short text and images to your Google Merchant Center catalog to drive deeper consideration. Start by reusing high-performing, inspirational imagery from existing social platforms to save time and showcase your brand at its best. Then, continue optimizing your creatives to improve relevance on YouTube and Google.

WHY IT MATTERS ? On average, advertisers see 33% more conversions at a similar cost per action (CPA) by adding product feeds to Demand Gen campaigns.

Evaluate and optimize performance

- **Adopt a test-and-learn strategy** as you fine-tune creatives for your unique audiences and goals. Check the insights in reporting tools to make informed decisions about creative optimization.

- Keep an eye on ad strength to understand how well you've built your ads to our specs. Once campaigns go live, review the engagement metrics (e. g. click-through rates) in asset reports to identify your top-performing assets, then swap out lower performers with new variations—make sure to aim for both quality *and* quantity.

- Review **segment by ad format reporting** to further diagnose how your ads are performing across key formats: YouTube Shorts, in-stream, and in-feed.

- Run A/B experiments for Demand Gen to test the effectiveness of your creatives across different surfaces by creating head-to-head tests in a clean environment.

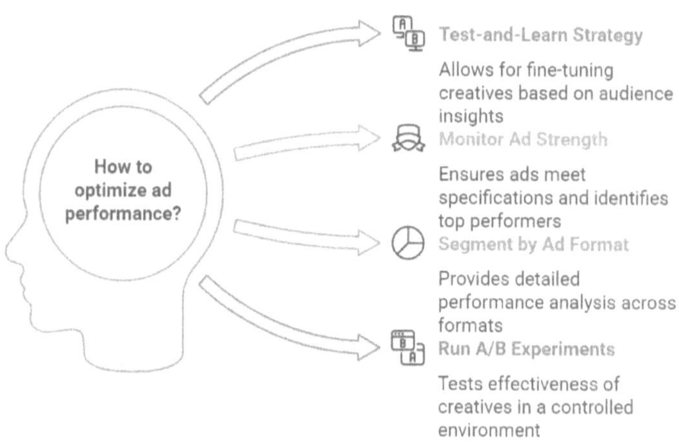

CASE STUDIES OF GEN AI USE FROM THE WORLD'S LEADING ORGANIZATIONS[19]

Since generative AI first captured the world's attention, there's been a vigorous discussion about what, exactly, the new technology is best used for. While we all enjoyed those early funny chats and witty limericks, we've quickly discovered that many of the biggest AI opportunities are clearly in the enterprise, government, and with exciting new companies.

In a matter of months, organizations have gone from AI helping answer questions, to AI making predictions, to generative AI agents. What makes AI agents unique is that they can take actions to achieve specific goals, whether that's guiding a shopper to the perfect pair of shoes, helping an employee looking for the right health benefits, or supporting nursing staff with smoother patient hand-offs during shifts changes. These aims are now being achieved through the AI agents they're developing in six key areas: customer service; employee empowerment; code creation; data analysis; cybersecurity; and creative ideation and production.

Six types of AI agents[50]

We continue to see customers and partners benefiting from AI agents — intelligent systems that go beyond simple chat and predictions, to proactively take actions. What makes AI agents unique is they help achieve specific goals, whether that's guiding a shopper to the perfect pair of shoes, helping an employee look for the right health benefits, or supporting nursing staff with smoother patient hand-offs during shift changes. We see AI agents centering around six use cases:

CUSTOMER AGENTS

Similar to great sales and service people, customer agents are able to listen carefully, understand your needs, and recommend the right products and services. They work seamlessly across channels including the web, mobile, and point of sale, and can be integrated into product experiences with voice and video.

Customer Agent Case Study: Dira by GoTo AI[24]

"GoTo Group" Company the "Company"), the largest digital ecosystem in Indonesia, has officially launched "Dira by GoTo AI", the first ever AI-enabled fintech voice assistant in Bahasa Indonesia.

GoTo is the largest digital ecosystem in Indonesia. GoTo's mission is to 'empower progress' by offering technology infrastructure and solutions that help everyone to access and thrive in the digital economy. The GoTo ecosystem provides a wide range of services including mobility, food delivery, groceries and logistics, as well as payments, financial services, and technology solutions for merchants. The ecosystem also provides e-commerce services through Tokopedia and banking services through its partnership with Bank Jago.

Dira is currently accessible on the GoPay app for a limited number of users and will be rolled out further before being made available on the Gojek app in the future. Dira by GoTo AI delivers a localized voice assistance solution. Dira is product developed by GoTo AI, a long term Artificial Intelligence (AI) innovation program that will develop and embed the latest AI technology throughout the GoTo ecosystem. Dira, short for Dikte Suara (voice dictation), has been designed to enhance the overall user experience, enabling users to discover GoPay app features with greater ease and perform various tasks faster using voice commands in Bahasa Indonesia.

Dira elevates user experience through simplicity and accessibility in the following ways:

1. Simplicity:

    a. Users can perform the same tasks with fewer steps. For example, accessing the "insurance bills" page to make social health insurance (BPJS) payments typically requires three clicks and a number of scrolls. With Dira, this same page can be reached in a single step through voice command.

b. Dira also simplifies navigation within the GoPay app, enabling users to discover new features and functions more easily by eliminating the need for manual typing or searching.

2. Accessibility:

Dira will make the benefits of AI more widely accessible as it does not add significantly to the size of the light-weight GoPay app, meaning it can be utilized on all types of mobile phones, including those with limited capacity, at no cost.

To access Dira on the GoPay app, users simply tap on the microphone icon on the top right corner of the GoPay app's main page. Users will then be able to directly give voice commands relating to multiple topics including electricity bill payments, money transfers, phone credit purchases, PIN change, and many more.

For enhanced safety and security, users will still be required to authenticate transactions with PIN and biometric verifications such as fingerprint or facial recognition. Without verification, users will not be able to complete any transactions.

Dira is a key innovation within the GoTo AI roadmap, which the Company will continue to develop as it enhances AI capabilities across the GoTo ecosystem. The roadmap is centered around three main areas; 1) creating a more seamless and convenient user experience, 2) strengthening safety across platforms, and 3) enhancing AI capacity and capability across GoTo.

(Know more at https://www. youtube. com/ watch?v=SEv_17tc9_Q.)

Customer Agent Case Study: ScottsMiracle-Gro[21]

ScottsMiracle-Gro developed an AI bot utilizing Vertex AI to deliver personalized gardening guidance and product suggestions for consumers. ScottsMiracle-Gro's consumer lawn and garden care products are accessible in prominent home centers, hardware stores, and various retail outlets around the nation. Due to the extensive range of its solutions, ScottsMiracle-Gro in-store field sales professionals are essential in educating retail partners and consumers about product choices, applications, and associated issues.

Historically, sales personnel have depended on a 450-page training manual for product information. The new AI-driven agent is available on mobile devices and enables colleagues to retrieve product information in real time. Users pose inquiries in natural language prompts and obtain comprehensive product information and guidance, which they may subsequently relay to in-store retail partners or consumers. An associate may inquire about the most suitable products considering the season and the consumer's specific growing conditions.

For instance, an associate can inquire about the best items depending on the time of year and the particular growing conditions of a customer. Consequently, ScottsMiracle-Gro sales associates are now equipped to offer consumers more significant product recommendations and guidance to enhance the overall customer experience. "At ScottsMiracle-Gro, we aim to provide our retail partners and consumers with superior lawn and garden products alongside optimal guidance. " Emily Wahl, vice president of Information Technology at ScottsMiracle-Gro, stated, "Google's robust generative AI solutions offer us a remarkable opportunity to transform how individuals interact with our brands and acquire knowledge about our products. ” “In summary, Google Cloud provides a genuine competitive advantage for us. ”

Customer Agent Case Study: World's Smartest Billboard" Campaign[41]:

The "World's Smartest Billboard" campaign for PODS, a moving and storage company, was Tombras' response to the Google AI Lighthouse program brief, which tasked agencies with utilizing Google AI to develop and implement an unfeasible campaign, rendered achievable by AI. In June, the involved agencies, including Tombras, presented their work at the Cannes International Festival of Creativity. The team requested Gemini for Google Workspace to identify key periods in the creative process where generative AI may provide significant contributions. Gemini's recommendations facilitated the cross-functional team in dismantling silos. The team trained Gemini using external data, including Google reviews, podcast transcripts, and industry reports, as well as internal data, such as client briefing transcripts, marketing data, and audience insights.

Upon acquiring that information, they instructed Gemini to produce a creative brief. Following the analysis of thousands of individual artifacts, Gemini generated 27 detailed pages of content. The subsequent step necessitated that creatives examine the paper to comprehend the extensive array of information available and collaborate with Gemini to develop the ideal brief. By concentrating on essential results, the team successfully re-engaged Gemini and condensed the brief to a targeted and actionable three pages. This brief-making highlighted the magnitude, speed, and capability of AI. To complete the extensive material required for the campaign, the team initially needed to establish the appropriate tone. "This was an endeavor to cultivate a novel voice," stated Baliga. "We desire it to be intelligent and highly perceptive, yet amicable." The creatives subsequently assumed the role as creative directors and endeavor to guide Gemini in its execution. The coaching manifested in several ways, including supplying example text and prompting Gemini to simulate the perspective of a 23-year-old residing in a specific location.

In addition to the role-playing prompts, Tombras utilized tools such as brand archetypes and existing copy samples to assist Gemini in generating the initial set of lines. The team utilized the finest elements from this group with additional supplies and urges to produce the subsequent outputs. The selections were utilized to motivate Gemini once more, resulting in 6, 000 lines that encapsulated the essence of the ad. On the activation day, the billboard displayed a minimum of five lines each neighborhood, each meticulously handpicked by a human expert. "We developed an API that integrates all headline data with real-time data and subsequently relays it to the truck for display, " stated Juan Tubert, chief technology officer of Tombras. The API resided on the Google Cloud Platform, integrating Vertex AI, Gemini, Maps, Sheets, and Cloud Run functionalities. Within 29 hours, the truck covered a total of 299 communities across the five boroughs, eliciting a remarkable response. PODS website sessions increased by 60%, while requests for quotes—a crucial performance metric—rose by 33% in the New York City region. The marketing results indicated the most significant weekly year-over-year increase in New York for the brand in years.

Customer Agent Case Study: Snap Inc. Partners with Google Cloud to Power Multi-Modal Generative AI Experiences Within its My AI Chatbot[48]

Initially introduced on Google Cloud in 2011, Snapchat provides a rapid and enjoyable method for visual communication with friends and family. The sustained appeal of these fundamental product values differentiates Snapchat from other online platforms and has facilitated its growth to over 850 million monthly active users.

As a pioneer in technology, Snap is shaping the role of generative AI in facilitating personal expression, enhancing global understanding, and fostering connections among friends and family. As the company persists in its investment in AI, Snap is already experiencing significant business value from its collaboration with Google Cloud. Following the implementation of Gemini on Vertex AI to enhance My AI, Snapchat experienced an engagement increase exceeding 2. 5 times in the United States.

Customer Agent Case Study: myVW app[13]

Volkswagen of America, Inc. functions as an operational division of Volkswagen Group of America, a subsidiary of Volkswagen AG. Volkswagen of America, based in Reston, Virginia, markets the Atlas, Atlas Cross Sport, Golf GTI, Golf R, ID. 4, Jetta, Jetta GLI, Taos, and Tiguan models via over 600 independent dealerships in the United States. The Volkswagen Group of America manages a cutting-edge assembly plant in Chattanooga, Tennessee, manufacturing Volkswagen brand vehicles such as the Atlas, Atlas Cross Sport, and ID. 4. The Volkswagen Group is a leading global manufacturer of passenger vehicles and the largest carmaker in Europe. Volkswagen is utilizing Google Cloud's premier AI and machine learning capabilities, along with the experience of Google Cloud Consulting, to enhance the myVW Virtual Assistant and offer car owners seamless access to essential vehicle information and services. The newly introduced generative AI-powered Virtual Assistant in the myVW app is now accessible to all My24 Atlas and Atlas Cross Sport car owners, enabling drivers to obtain information and answers pertinent to their vehicles.

The myVW Virtual Assistant integrates Volkswagen's linked car data with Gemini models on Google Cloud's Vertex AI platform to provide consumers with low-latency, precise information. Owners of the Atlas and Atlas Cross Sport can utilize the new Virtual Assistant via the myVW app to navigate their owners' manuals and inquire about topics such as, "How do I replace a flat tire?" or "What is the significance of this digital cockpit indicator light?" Furthermore, myVW app users can utilize Gemini's multi-modal functionalities to access pertinent information and context regarding indicator lights by only directing their smartphone cameras at their dashboards.

By integrating Google Cloud's Vertex AI with BigQuery, Volkswagen can calibrate and refine Gemini models using various data sources, such as vehicle owner's manuals, customer FAQs, help center articles, official Volkswagen YouTube videos, and instructional guides. Volkswagen utilized the knowledge of Google Cloud Consulting during the whole app development process, encompassing design and implementation. This extensive support guarantees that the app fulfills Volkswagen's precise regulatory obligations and elevated standards while providing an innovative and user-focused experience.

Customer Agent Case Study: Alaska Airlines[47]:

Alaska Airlines is creating a natural language search system that offers travelers a conversational experience driven by AI, similar to engaging with an informed travel advisor. This chatbot seeks to optimize travel reservations, improve consumer satisfaction, and strengthen brand recognition. A flyer can instruct the tool, "I wish to vacation in the mountains for four days in July within a budget. " The AI engine will thereafter provide recommendations for Alaska flights originating from the traveler's city. Users can click on an information button to receive an explanation on the selection of specific flights and destinations.

Customer Agent Case Study: Bennie Health[51]:

Bennie Health leverages Google Cloud's Vertex AI to drive its employee health benefits platform, utilizing its machine learning capabilities to analyze data, provide actionable insights, and streamline the process of managing employee healthcare benefits, ultimately enhancing decision-making for both employees and HR teams.

Key points about this application:

- **Platform enhancement:** Vertex AI helps Bennie Health improve the functionality of their employee health benefits platform by offering advanced data analysis and personalized recommendations.

- **Data-driven insights:** By processing large datasets, the AI can generate valuable insights regarding employee health trends, helping companies tailor their benefit plans accordingly.

- **Streamlined decision-making:** The platform powered by Vertex AI aims to simplify the process of choosing health plans for employees, making it more efficient for both individuals and HR personnel.

Customer Agent Case Study: CareerVillage[15]

CareerVillage is a nonprofit entity that democratizes access to career information and coaching, especially for underserved youth and adults. CareerVillage equips individuals to confidently explore their career paths through new tools and collaborations. CareerVillage introduced Coach, an innovative AI career development tool for marginalized adolescents and adults. The coach's development entailed collaboration with over twenty educational institutions, organizations, and workforce boards, and was evaluated by more than 900 students and educators. The Coach platform distinguishes itself among AI career aids due to its research-supported impact assessment. It employs the validated CAAS-SF survey to monitor learners' career preparedness advancement, in conjunction with mini-surveys evaluating the efficacy of specific activities. This data enhances student experiences and aids career preparedness research, potentially enhancing the entire sector.

Customer Agent Case Study: Character. ai[23]

Character. AI is an innovative chatbot firm founded by former Google developers Noam Shazeer and Daniel De Freitas. They have developed an impressive platform for interacting with AI-driven personas known as "Characters. " These characters may be renowned individuals, historical personalities, fictional characters, or those of your own invention. Character. ai developed their realistic conversational chat platform with the comprehensive suite of Google Cloud AI services for model training and everyday operations, enabling it to handle terabytes of interactions daily without disruption. Character. AI significantly surpasses ChatGPT in user engagement, with an average visit duration of 26.5 minutes compared to ChatGPT's 7.4 minutes. In January, character. ai traffic increased by 1,997,496% compared to the previous year.

Customer Agent Case Study: Formula E Racing[28]

Formula E racing, established in 2012, aims to demonstrate the potential of sustainable transportation by promoting electric vehicles in the pursuit of a cleaner future. Similar to Formula 1 racing, Formula E is a motorsport featuring rapid, streamlined race cars, however powered by batteries. Formula E is dedicated to showcasing the efficacy of electric vehicles as a remedy for urban air pollution while simultaneously dismantling obstacles within the electric vehicle sector.

Research indicates that cognitive diversity enhances problem-solving, while a diverse collaborative ecology, both internal and external, further amplifies this effect. Formula E has embraced that principle. A few tenths of a second frequently dictate race results. It is significantly more competitive than the majority of sports, and any minor oversight can preclude victory.

Similar to its significance in the corporate sector, big data has become an essential competitive advantage in Formula E. Sylvain Filippi, Managing Director and CTO of Envision, states, "If we lose the data, we lose the competition."

Races are frequently determined by mere fractions of a second, rendering data analytics a crucial element in Formula E. Drivers dedicate extensive hours to the simulator in preparation for each race. Advanced analytics allow drivers to analyze each lap, discern strengths and areas for improvement, and enhance their racing strategies.

The qualification and the race occur on the same day, allowing only a few hours to examine vast quantities of data from the numerous sensors on each vehicle. The Envision team may now make improved and expedited decisions during the race by employing radio analytics, a tool that analyzes radio communications between competing drivers and their engineers, processing this unstructured data into pertinent segments to derive insights. These findings inform pivotal decisions throughout a race. The team used AI to identify trends during the season, utilizing their Lap Estimate Optimizer (LEO), an AI-driven scenario engine. LEO delivers race-day analysis during pivotal events, such safety car interruptions, alterations in on-track conditions, or assaults from competing vehicles. Analysts recently assessed the ramifications of a hailstorm, and its impacts were integrated into the strategy.

Fan involvement serves as a crucial metric of performance in Formula E. In the future, Envision will utilize AI to provide the team with a comprehensive grasp of the whole Formula E fan demographic via their forthcoming Fan 360 initiative. Similar to how corporations analyze the consumer experience, Formula E employs data analytics to develop a cohesive fan engagement strategy. Utilizing insights is essential for high-performance teams in contemporary organizations. Envision engages in this activity consistently throughout both the racing season and the off-season.

Despite a successful race weekend, a call occurs two days later in which the team solely addresses the shortcomings. The team asserts that when operating at 97% or 98%, achieving 99.95% is desired.

Customer Agent Case Study: General Motors' OnStar[27]:

General Motors and Google Cloud have announced fresh specifics of their collaboration to integrate conversational AI technology into millions of GM vehicles, assisting drivers in numerous capacities. Since its inception in 2022, GM's OnStar Interactive Virtual Assistant (IVA) has utilized sophisticated intent-recognition algorithms backed by Google Cloud's conversational AI technologies, offering OnStar Members answers to frequently asked questions, along with routing and navigation support. The effective implementation of Google Cloud's AI in GM's OnStar service has paved the way for future collaborative generative AI initiatives between GM and Google Cloud.

GM's intention to partner with Google Cloud in investigating comprehensive generative AI applications is a continuation of the collaboration initiated in 2019, when GM integrated Google technology into its inaugural vehicles. Since that time, the quantity of GM vehicles equipped with integrated Google technology has increased, providing customers with direct access to Google Assistant, Google Maps, and Google Play via their vehicles' central screens. The partnership subsequently extended to the implementation of Google Cloud's conversational AI platform, Dialogflow. Utilizing this technology, GM's OnStar virtual assistant now manages over 1 million customer requests monthly in the U.S. and Canada, and is accessible in the majority of model year 2015 and newer GM vehicles equipped with OnStar.

GM's OnStar Interactive Virtual Assistant (IVA), introduced in 2022, employs sophisticated AI-driven intent detection technologies with Google Cloud's Dialogflow to offer OnStar Members routing and navigation support, including turn-by-turn directions. The OnStar IVA aids with typical inquiries begun via the non-emergency OnStar blue button in GM vehicles, while also striving to identify phrases and words that may indicate an emergency, facilitating prompt connection to OnStar's specially qualified emergency Advisors.

This technology enables OnStar to promptly comprehend a customer's inquiry or request upon initial articulation, delivering an answer in a contemporary, natural-sounding voice. Customers recognize the consistent OnStar "voice" whether they are in their vehicle or on a phone call, and they have responded well to experiences that do not involve hold times. The OnStar IVA has effectively assisted GM customers seeking navigation support, allowing OnStar Advisors to dedicate more time to customers with inquiries necessitating a personal touch.

Furthermore, GM is utilizing Google Cloud's Dialogflow technology to develop chatbots that can interactively address consumer inquiries regarding GM vehicles and product features, drawing on the technical information from GM's comprehensive vehicle data repositories. This technology enables clients to obtain prompt responses to inquiries such as, "Provide details about GM's 2024 EV lineup, " or discover how to utilize new technological capabilities in their automobile. These chatbots operate on GM's corporate and car brand websites, providing enhanced ease for customers seeking specialized vehicle-related information.

GM's initiative to integrate Dialogflow into its OnStar system will garner attention within the technology sector at Google Cloud's annual Next event in San Francisco. In a very competitive landscape of enterprises utilizing Google Cloud technology, GM distinguished itself by its extensive and effective implementation of AI, resulting in a "Talent Transformation" award.

Customer Agent Case Study: GroupBy's eCommerce Search and Product Discovery Platform[9]:

Established in 2013, GroupBy is a SaaS technology solution specializing in eCommerce search and product discovery, serving prominent B2B and B2C businesses. GroupBy's AI-centric composable platform is introducing advanced search technologies to retailers globally, facilitating the connection between consumers and merchants. The platform, powered by Google Cloud Vertex AI Search for Retail, includes Data Enrichment, Search and Recommendations, Merchandising, and Analytics and Reporting, offering eCommerce merchants a robust suite of products and services aimed at improving the digital customer experience. The GroupBy platform, also known as "RS", is founded on AI principles, is revolutionizing eCommerce merchandising from a rule-based approach to a revenue-generating model, enhancing productivity and efficiency while decreasing time to market. This enables retailers, wholesalers, and distributors to concentrate on strategic business initiatives that enhance revenue.

RS is pioneering the use of GroupBy's Product Discovery Platform, enhanced by Google Cloud's advanced search engine, in the industrial manufacturing sector. The search engine that underpins GroupBy's platform utilizes Google's extensive experience in providing tailored information across its primary services, including Google Search, Google Shopping, and YouTube. Equipped with substantially more data than conventional legacy systems, advanced machine learning (ML) and artificial intelligence (AI) exhibit an enhanced comprehension of human intent and context. Consequently, RS can now provide pertinent, purchasable, and tailored search results targeted for revenue across both long-tail and broad search queries, encompassing specialty industry terminology, which constitutes the majority of RS's search traffic. This AI-driven search optimization allows RS to autonomously elevate cold-start products from emerging brands and highlight offerings from lesser businesses, guaranteeing that the most pertinent products are displayed for each search query.

Following the transition to GroupBy's AI-driven search and product discovery platform, RS has transformed its merchandising procedures from a rule-based system to a revenue-generating business. The AI capability has allowed the organization to effectively eradicate over 30,000 search rules, resulting in a productivity enhancement above 60%. Equipping RS with a tool that facilitates an optimal equilibrium between AI-driven optimization and manual curation allows their internal merchandising teams to concentrate more on campaign development, inventory transparency, and the integration of new technologies that will elevate their performance.

RS's achievements with the GroupBy Search and Product Discovery Platform, along with robust internationalization capabilities enhanced by Google's translation technology, have led to the decision to extend the search platform's integration to more APAC markets for imminent deployment. This system enables RS to efficiently manage multilingual information, providing pertinent search results for non-English inquiries.

EMPLOYEE AGENTS

Employee agents help workers be more productive and collaborate better together. These agents can streamline processes, manage repetitive tasks, answer employee questions, as well as edit and translate critical communications.

Employee Agent Case Study: Bell Canada and Google Cloud power an AI-driven contact centre revolution.

Bell is the largest communications firm in Canada, offering sophisticated broadband Internet, wireless, television, media, and corporate communication services nationwide. Established in Montréal in 1880, Bell is entirely owned by BCE Inc.

Bell Canada deployed Google Cloud Contact Center AI (CCAI) for Canadian enterprises. Google Cloud's CCAI from Bell is a managed solution enhanced by professional services expertise, facilitating an intelligent experience for both customers and agents with generative AI technology. Google CCAI from Bell delivers comprehensive conversational experiences and analytics, offering scalability and flexibility that can be integrated into current contact center infrastructures and cloud contact centers of any magnitude. Google's CCAI solutions can yield remarkable results, as evidenced by Bell's deployment experience. Bell will collaborate with clients to tailor use cases that utilize the advanced technical solutions offered by Google CCAI through Bell, including:

- Virtual Agent — Conversational virtual agents diminish contact volumes and expedite resolution times by gathering essential information to address straightforward consumer inquiries, so allowing human agents to manage more intricate problems. When clients require assistance from an agent, they will be promptly connected and automatically routed to the agent possessing the appropriate skills to address their concern.

- Agent Assistance – Agent Assist functions as a virtual supervisor, employing real-time natural language processing to assess client demands and sentiment, while providing sequential recommendations to enable agents to deliver optimal responses and solutions with assurance. Accelerated agent onboarding, enhanced customer experience, less callbacks for same issues, and increased revenue are demonstrated results of Agent Assist.

- Analytics and Insights - Pragmatic insights on customer experience and sentiment enable managers and agents to derive lessons from each interaction. Analyses of interactions enhance comprehension of company patterns, interaction catalysts, traffic, and other essential data. Insights facilitate strategic business decisions, customized agent coaching, and lead to enhanced data-driven workforce planning and management.

Bell is implementing both virtual agent and contact center as a service AI solutions (CCAI and CCAIP) within its contact centers, digitally transforming and enhancing their internal systems, thereby improving customer experiences for Bell clients and assisting them in cultivating expertise to support Canadian businesses with their integrations. Bell offers clients comprehensive managed support, encompassing solution assessment, customer journey mapping and optimization, workforce management, quality assurance, technology and applied AI integrations, as well as enhancements to agent experience and change management.

Bell provides augmented proficiency on Google Cloud. Bell will incorporate Google CCAI technologies into its Contact Centre Practice, which has a demonstrated history of successful premise and cloud contact centre operations, emphasizing customer happiness. By utilizing these solutions internally, the Professional and Managed Services teams are acquiring substantial knowledge and expertise to successfully assist the customers during the digital transition of their contact centers. By minimizing agent training duration and providing tools to enhance sales performance, Google CCAI, in collaboration with Bell, seeks to transform a conventional cost center into a revenue-generating entity. The introduction of Google CCAI marks a pivotal achievement for Bell as the company persists in aiding Canadian enterprises in their digital transformation endeavors with advanced solutions. Bell is implementing a comprehensive digital transformation and, with Google CCAI services, is introducing additional solutions within its contact centers, including the Google Cloud Contact Centre AI Platform.

Employee Agent Case Study:Dun & Bradstreet[25]:

Dun & Bradstreet, a premier global supplier of business decision-making data and analytics, empowers enterprises worldwide to enhance their company performance. Dun & Bradstreet's Data Cloud drives solutions and provides insights that enable customers to enhance revenue, reduce costs, minimize risks, and change their enterprises. It is a premier international supplier of business decision-making data and analytics. The organization has deployed SmartMail AI and SmartSearch AI. The newly integrated Generative Artificial Intelligence (Gen AI) capabilities in D&B Hoovers enhance the company's previously established Gen AI solutions from the last year.

D&B Hoovers SmartMail AI and SmartSearch AI enhance sales prospecting and lead generation across many channels, refine targeting and personalization to create more sophisticated customer experiences, and offer a seamless and efficient experience for sales and marketing teams. Client feedback has indicated improvements in productivity, process simplification, and market entry speed. Presently, 4, 000 customers are using these new AI-driven capabilities, reflecting Dun & Bradstreet's client engagement and its continuous innovation to address their requirements. D&B Hoovers SmartMail AI and SmartSearch AI are constructed on AiBE, Dun & Bradstreet's core framework for the rapid development, evaluation, and deployment of new solutions.

Hoovers SmartMail AI optimizes the outreach process by automating message and deploying it to highly targeted contacts. A productivity enhancer for sales and marketing teams, it utilizes AI-optimized messaging for personalized content generation, including emails to prospects and customers. SmartMail AI utilizes personalized information regarding the contact and their relationship with the sender, modifies the wording in up to 19 languages worldwide, adjusts the email tone, and prepares the message for direct transmission from the sender's email program. Hoovers SmartSearch AI is an artificial intelligence-driven chat assistant that enables users to efficiently create focused lists of firms and connections based on certain criteria, including country, city, industry, company size, and additional parameters. This interactive feature guarantees the delivery of the user's intended audience to optimize reach and reaction depending on metrics, facilitating the identification and execution of targeted opportunities.

Employee Agent Case Study:England's Football Association[32]:

As part of its preparations for the Euro 2024 tournament, the Football Association of England has entered into a collaboration with Google Cloud in order to receive essential insights from the latter. The Scouting Summarizations project is being developed by the Football Association in conjunction with Google Cloud. This project will make use of generative artificial intelligence technologies. In spite of the fact that the captain of the team, who was also responsible for England's advancement to the semifinals of the 2018 World Cup, continues to travel across the country in order to personally monitor players, the Player Profiling System offers him with a powerful instrument.

All of the participants are under the watchful eye of the association managers throughout each and every match that their respective club does. According to the information that they acquire from these performances, they are able to make well-informed decisions by analyzing the performance of the players in comparison to particular opponents as well as the trends that the team has been experiencing.

In order to find areas of the team that have room for improvement, data analysis is an extremely helpful tool. Although there is no alternative for good coaching, the association contends that the exploitation of data and technology can offer teams with an advantage. This is despite the fact that there is no substitute for professional coaching.

The program known as Football Association Scouting Summarizations, which makes use of Vertex AI to examine thousands of previous scouting reports on players at all levels, is still in its early stages of development. It is possible to assign a numerical value to the implicit and expert knowledge that a scout owns. Therefore, a grade is given to them for each competition that they participate in. A collection of scores is produced as a consequence of this over time. When a scout is playing a game, the wisdom and insight that they possess are reduced to a numerical value, which makes the insights extremely simplified.

Employee Agent Case Study:Hiscox[12]:

Hiscox, a worldwide insurance expert, collaborated with Google Cloud to develop the nation's first artificial intelligence (AI)-enhanced lead underwriting model for the London Market insurance business.

In order to automate lead algorithmic underwriting from the submission to the quotation stage, the cooperation merges the generative artificial intelligence technology of Google Cloud with the technological platform that Hiscox London Market has recently created, Hiscox AI Laboratories (Hailo).

The task included the utilization of the Vertex AI platform as well as the BigQuery service offered by Google Cloud in order to extract vital data and insights from the submissions of emails. Within the framework of the existing insurance business model, this procedure is often carried out manually and can take up to three days to complete. Using artificial intelligence (AI) in certain aspects of the underwriting process, underwriting teams are able to provide estimates in as little as three minutes.

Employee Agent Case Study:Quantum Metric[45]

Quantum Metric is the digital analytics platform that is customer-centric and designed for the most prominent organizations of the present day. The Quantum Metric platform offers a comprehensive understanding of customers that is quantified and linked to core business objectives, as well as a simplified approach to monitoring, diagnosing, and optimizing the digital journeys that are most important. Currently, Quantum Metric is able to acquire insights from 45% of the global internet user population, thereby enabling global brands in all industries to more effectively and quickly understand their customers. Quantum Metric has introduced Felix AI, a new generation of artificial intelligence-powered session summarization that is enabled by Google Cloud's Gemini Pro. Felix AI leverages the capabilities of Google Gemini to offer a level of clarity regarding the digital experience.

Quantum Metric has developed a Gen AI-powered product that leverages their extensive customer-centric data set to assist their customers in expediting their AI strategy. With Felix AI at the disposal of digital leaders, customers can revolutionize the manner in which teams analyze and empathize with consumer opportunities. Session replays, which are frequently implemented by digital organizations, offer essential insight into the consumer experience; however, they are inherently time-consuming and intricate. In fact, Quantum Metric customers devoted more than 320K hours to the evaluation of session data in 2023. Felix AI summarizes a session in seconds, capturing the precise experience the visitor went through, powered by Google Cloud's Gemini Pro model. Felix AI provides a simplified approach to digital customer listening that can be instantly quantified to understand the scale of each issue and its impact on key business metrics, breaking away from the traditional session replay tools. Felix's prompt offers users the opportunity to inquire about the specifics of an individual's experience, including the campaign from which the consumer originated.

Felix AI can be expanded to the channels and use cases that digital teams require the most, such as:

- Direct integrations into VoC feedback received via text, email, or Slack, providing immediate context on customer feedback.

- Role-based summaries, which include support for the call center, enable agents to immediately comprehend the customer's issue prior to their explanation.

Felix AI provides Quantum Metric teams with the ability to simplify the process of listening to their consumers, as well as the tools to listen at scale and across the entire customer lifecycle, such as Interactions and User Analytics.

CODE AGENTS

Code agents assist developers and product teams in designing, creating, and operating applications more efficiently, while also facilitating the acquisition of new programming languages and codebases. Numerous firms are currently experiencing double-digit increases in productivity, resulting in expedited deployment and more refined, lucid code.

Code Agent Case Study:Labelbox[30]:

Labelbox serves as the data factory for generative AI, supplying superior, distinctive data to prominent model developers and enterprise AI teams. Labelbox's extensive platform integrates on-demand expert labeling services with a premier data labeling platform. Labelbox's software-centric methodology provides unparalleled quality, control, and efficiency, while the labeling services leverage the wide and sophisticated expertise of the Alignerr expert community to achieve high throughput and minimal reaction times. Labelbox's clientele comprises Fortune 500 corporations and prominent AI laboratories.

Labelbox realized that as Large Language Models (LLMs) become more sophisticated, accurately evaluating their performance becomes increasingly critical. While automated metrics provide insights, human evaluation remains the gold standard for understanding nuances like relevance, bias, and overall quality. However, conducting large-scale, high-quality human evaluations is a major challenge for most enterprises, requiring significant time, resources, and expertise.

Labelbox partnered with Google Cloud to deliver a fully managed LLM evaluation solution directly integrated into the Vertex AI platform. This solution empowers Google Cloud customers to seamlessly launch human evaluation jobs, set specific criteria for evaluation (e.g. question-answering, summarization).

Customers can now develop and ship LLM applications with confidence. They receive high-quality results within days. Launching LLM evaluation jobs takes minutes.

Vertex AI customers can utilize the LLM Evaluation solution to initiate an evaluation job directly within the Vertex AI interface, select their preferred evaluation type (e. g. , single model or side-by-side comparison) and criteria (e. g. , question-answer, multi-turn chat, summarization), and receive quality-reviewed results from experienced evaluators within days.

Labelbox's LLM evaluation service offers teams convenient access to human evaluators who assess the efficacy of their organization's LLMs based on a diverse array of customized criteria, including instruction adherence, verbosity, and response relevancy.

Through linked APIs, users can effortlessly configure their tasks within the Vertex AI platform, with all subsequent processes managed by Labelbox prior to quality assurance. The seamless presentation of the labeling team's responses within the Vertex AI platform enables customers to assess and accept results, so ensuring complete control over annotation quality.

DATA AGENTS

Data agents function as accessible, proficient data analysts and researchers. They can assist in addressing inquiries regarding internal and external sources, synthesizing information, formulating new models, and, most importantly, identifying questions we have yet to consider and then providing answers.

Data Agent Case Study:Bayer Crop Science[6]:

Bayer is a multinational corporation specializing in the life sciences, particularly in health care and nutrition. Aligned with its vision, "Health for all, Hunger for none, " the company's offerings are crafted to enhance the well-being of individuals and the earth by addressing the significant issues posed by an expanding and aging global populace. Bayer is dedicated to promoting sustainable development and creating a beneficial impact through its enterprises. The Group seeks to enhance its profitability and generate value through innovation and expansion. The Bayer brand embodies trust, trustworthiness, and quality globally. In fiscal year 2023, the Group employed over 100, 000 individuals and had sales of 47. 6 billion euros. Research and Development expenditures, excluding special items, totaled 5. 8 billion euros.

Bayer introduced Climate FieldView™ functionalities to assist customers in transitioning from the 2024 harvest to the 2025 planning phase. FieldView serves as the premier product of Climate LLC, the digital agriculture division of Bayer. Initially introduced in the United States and Canada, FieldView is currently accessible in 23 countries across over 250 million subscribed acres, offering farmers enhanced insights into their fields to facilitate informed operational decisions aimed at optimizing yields, maximizing efficiency, and mitigating risk. The newly developed capabilities enhance comprehension of the effects of seed, fertility, and crop protection sprays on yield, while enabling farmers and their trusted advisors to swiftly obtain useful information "at a glance. "

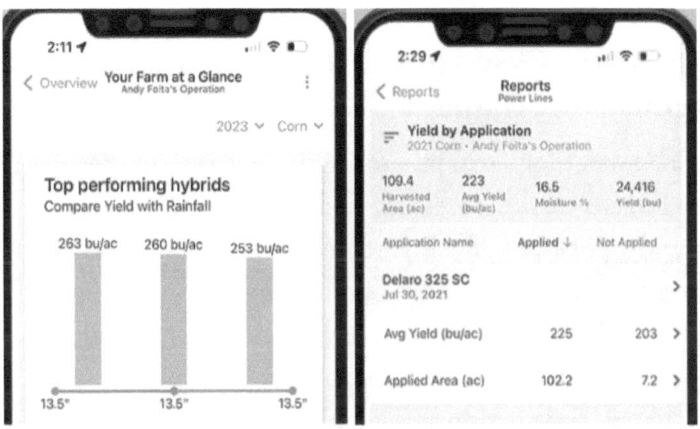

Historically, farmers have had to analyze their data to identify trends, outliers, and opportunities. This may be laborious and time-intensive. Your Farm at a Glance is an innovative tool that delivers a concise overview of farm operations and promptly highlights critical information, like harvest progress, average moisture and yield, top-performing hybrids and types, as well as the highest and lowest performing fields.

Your Farm at a Glance eliminates unnecessary clicks by offering a concise summary overview, whereas Yield Analysis by Application enables clients to conduct a more in-depth examination of their data. A field-level study of the diverse crop protection and fertility products utilized over the season enables consumers to assess product effectiveness and return on investment more effectively.

Upon initiation by their agricultural clients, dealers and retail advisors can additionally obtain information from both Your

Farm at a Glance and Yield Analysis by Application. Bayer always attends to user feedback and provides enhancements that elevate the FieldView experience.

Data Agent Case Study: AI in Construction Engineering: Gamuda Berhad[51]

As a developing nation, Malaysia persists in constructing new infrastructures to satisfy industrial demands. The nation currently possesses the highest number of skyscrapers in the region and shows no signs of diminishing its construction efforts. Additionally, Malaysia is currently developing new rail networks to link the capital with additional cities throughout. Although other large construction and engineering firms exist in Malaysia, Gamuda Berhad has been utilizing technology in its operations for an extended period. Gamuda has recently unveiled expansion plans in collaboration with Google Cloud to provide enterprise-grade generative AI capabilities to all employees, enabling them to execute engineering, construction, and public infrastructure projects in the region more effectively and innovatively. The Gamuda Innovation Hub is pioneering a digital and data-centric methodology for building while enhancing skills in Google Cloud capabilities. Gamuda established the Gamuda Digital Operating System (GDOS) to implement generative AI, creating a standardized ecosystem of tools for all Gamuda projects, wherein company data is aggregated and supported by a unified data cloud platform. This encompasses data from essential systems such as Autodesk Construction Cloud and SAP S4/HANA. This follows the successful move of Gamuda's SAP S4/HANA systems from Amazon Web Services (AWS) to Google Cloud in 2023, facilitated by Google Cloud partner Cloudspace.

Transferring all compute workloads, including SAP S4/HANA, to Google Cloud permitted the organization to consolidate computation and data into a singular cloud platform, thereby allowing the team to concentrate on value-generating use cases and diverting attention from infrastructure management. Google Cloud's BigQuery data warehouse and workload-optimized architecture provided cost efficiencies, enabling enhanced value extraction from their data assets.

A consolidated data cloud offers Gamuda's design, engineering, finance, supply chain, and field operations teams a comprehensive, integrated, and real-time perspective of all project workflows. This facilitates agile, data-informed decision-making during the execution of intricate, long-term projects in Malaysia, Australia, Singapore, and Taiwan. To protect its company data and essential digital systems, Gamuda has adopted Google Cloud's Security Command Center Premium platform, which utilizes machine learning for enhanced threat detection and prevention, attack path simulation, and maintaining regulatory compliance. One initiative that thoroughly explores Gamuda's tunneling expertise is the implementation of Google Cloud's Gemini models on the Vertex AI platform to develop and incorporate a generative AI-driven conversational agent into its cloud-based Tunnel Insight platform, with assistance from CloudMile, a Google Cloud partner.

Tunnel Insight, utilizing Google Cloud, processes, displays, and analyzes sensor data from the inaugural autonomous tunnel boring machines (A-TBMs) created internally by Gamuda. Utilizing advanced algorithms to automate repetitive operational tasks such as machine steering and muck excavation, these A-TBMs are employed for enhanced tunneling in construction projects, including the Defu and West Coast Mass Rapid Transit stations and tunnels in Singapore, as well as the Sydney Metro West-Western Tunnelling Package in Australia. The extensive data generated by these operations can hinder workers from swiftly extracting insights for prompt responses to geological changes or maintenance requirements. The generative AI-driven conversational agent is used by personnel to swiftly retrieve pertinent summaries and directives from an extensive database of machine documentation, facilitating the maintenance procedure and enabling the straightforward interpretation of data charts on machine performance in natural language.

Gamuda has utilized Vertex AI Search and Conversation to develop generative search and conversation solutions for its market intelligence, design, and technical teams. These staff can now condense thousands of pages of study documentation into succinct summaries within minutes and extract data from numerous past projects for insights to guide new project contract submissions.

Data Agent Case Study: Research and Consulting: Ipsos[38]

Since transitioning its panel surveys online in 2001, the worldwide market research and consultancy organization has consistently used new technology and methodology to enhance productivity and client value proposition.

The most significant asset for decision-making in a dynamic environment is precise data pertinent to companies implementing strategic goals. Paris-based Ipsos has adeptly armed over 5,000 clients with insights to confidently navigate a rapidly transforming world. For decades, dependence on technology has been essential.

The digital transformation process of Ipsos can be categorized into many stages, each characterized by certain aims and challenges. The initial implementation commenced in 2001 when it transitioned its panels and surveys to an online format, thereby decreasing expenses and enhancing the efficiency and breadth of data collection. In 2002, the corporation commenced the online dissemination of its expertise to consumers through dashboards and interactive reports, facilitating more efficient and expedited access to data and analysis. The digitization of internal processes occurred in 2011, when the organization opted to enhance its internal data management, quality control, project management, and communication through digital tools and platforms. Four years later, the firm utilized Microsoft Office 365, enhancing communication and productivity among employees, partners, and customers globally.

In 2018, Ipsos advanced its transformation by launching a comprehensive end-to-end service capability for packaged research via its digital platform, enabling clients to plan, execute, and assess their own research projects utilizing Ipsos' expertise and resources. In 2023, AI-powered Insights Delivery was launched to revolutionize the company's operations and the provision of insights to clients. They employed huge language models to produce innovative insights, utilizing AI capabilities, augmented by data science models, and customized to the provided services.

Ipsos's recent digital transformation initiative involves transitioning its reporting and analytics to a standardized digital delivery platform utilizing a cloud-enabled infrastructure and a proprietary reporting engine based on open standards. The initiative employs agile approaches to deliver expedited and enhanced outcomes to clients.

A primary advantage of this project is consistency, since Ipsos can guarantee uniform results across various countries, sectors, and services by adhering to identical standards and best practices. Flexibility is another advantage, as it enables the brand to tailor its offerings to the distinct demands and preferences of each client, employing various formats, languages, and visualizations. Scalability via cloud computing facilitates the management of substantial data quantities and intricate analyses without sacrificing performance or quality. To achieve success in these creative areas, Ipsos collaborates with premier cloud providers to utilize their infrastructure, services, and experience. In certain instances, it collaborates with certain integrators, including Accenture and Thoughtworks, to facilitate the implementation and integration of solutions. Ipsos regards digital transformation as a strategic need for development and competitiveness. They utilize cloud-scale technologies and proprietary data science and analytics engines constructed on open standards to manage extensive data volumes. Among the technologies employed by Ipsos, cloud computing is prominent, utilizing services from Microsoft Azure, Google Cloud Platform, and AWS for infrastructure, storage, processing, analytic, and artificial intelligence requirements.

The company has created a proprietary reporting engine that offers sophisticated statistical analysis, interactive dashboards, and reports, utilizing open standards including HTML5, CSS3, JavaScript, D3. js, and React. js.

Another technological advancement is a data science engine that conducts sophisticated analysis and modeling, utilizing open standards such as Python, R, TensorFlow, and PyTorch. Ultimately, it employs LLMs such as GPT-4 to produce natural language insights from data through AI methodologies, including natural language processing and generation The company intends to initiate additional digital transformation initiatives aimed at utilizing LLMs to provide advanced insights to clients. The company asserts that LLMs possess the capability to transform the research sector by providing swifter, more profound, and pertinent insights from data. Consequently, Ipsos has initiated initiatives focused on sentiment analysis of customers and interest groups utilizing several sources, including social media, opinions, surveys, and interviews. This technique is utilized to condense extensive material from news stories, reports, documents, and transcripts, in addition to generating fresh content for diverse applications such as headlines, captions, descriptions, and suggestions.

Data Agent Case Study: Data in Healthcare Business: Mendel[5]

Mendel is a pioneering artificial intelligence (AI) firm dedicated to accelerating that process more than ever. Mendel, in collaboration with Amazon Web Services (AWS), is employing AI to address the deficiencies of conventional healthcare technologies and processes that hinder clinical inquiry. Mendel's AI interprets clinical data with clinician-like reasoning by indexing both organized and unstructured data, allowing healthcare professionals to interact with patient information through natural language communication.

Mendel was co-founded by Karim Galil and Wael Salloum in 2017, initiating their venture in a two-person office in Silicon Valley. After five years and substantial investment in research and development, Mendel's inaugural model was introduced. Currently, the company is the most capitalized clinical natural language processing (NLP) innovator in its sector, employing over 100 individuals and boasting a clientele that includes some of the foremost life sciences enterprises globally.

The primary challenge facing healthcare businesses today is the abundance of data, the majority of which is unstructured and not searchable. Numerous healthcare systems employ various electronic medical records (EMRs), each encompassing segments of the comprehensive patient experience. Mendel integrates disparate and unstructured data into a unified, coherent patient journey. Mendel interprets the data, allowing healthcare workers to effectively communicate with medical records. The platform features an AI co-pilot store that allows clients to obtain AI co-pilots for various workflows. They also empower their clients to create their own AI co-pilots. Mendel is enhancing patient care by providing healthcare workers with AI-powered solutions to address the deficiencies of current systems and processes. Mendel's technology allows end users to engage with data through natural language. For instance, the patient records may be composed in English, yet it is not straightforward English; rather, it employs very complex terminology. Fatigue may serve as both a symptom and a side effect. This may lead to shallow reasoning and hallucinations that could have significant repercussions in therapeutic environments.

Rules-based systems are likewise inadequate. These technologies fail to mimic the nuanced judgment and adaptive learning of human therapists, hence lacking a comprehensive grasp of patient care. This inflexibility is incongruent with the dynamic nature of medical knowledge and practice. Mendel has created a hybrid methodology for clinical reasoning that integrates deep learning with symbolic AI techniques. Its AI systems possess the ability to read, reason, and emulate a physician's comprehension of clinical language. Mendel's platform consists of clinical reasoning models that provide complaint intelligence from millions of patients, integrated with advanced NLP models that perform various functions. This encompasses optical character recognition (OCR), document segmentation, document classification, named entity extraction, relation extraction, de-identification, and retrieval and generation based on large language models (LLMs).

Mendel is utilizing the AWS Migration Acceleration Program (MAP) to optimize and facilitate the migration process. It fundamentally facilitates expedited and lower-risk migration for businesses. The initiative offers resources that save expenses and expedite outcomes, in addition to customized training materials, expertise from the AWS Partner Network (APN), and AWS funding.

The Mendel team is presently engaged on pre-training a foundational model designed to provide clinical oncology content. In addition to knowledge, Mendel required a cloud partner proficient in securely keeping patient data in strict adherence to regulatory requirements and regional legislation, such as the Health Insurance Portability and Accountability Act (HIPAA). Privacy is a significant concern in healthcare. The storage and management of information is a necessity for any healthcare startup. AWS has assisted Mendel in enhancing and advancing their security posture using established best practices and innovative technology. Mendel is planning to persist in empowering healthcare professionals and enhancing patient care using AI on AWS. The organization is now investigating the capabilities of AWS Trainium and AWS Inferentia chips to enhance performance and decrease expenses related to its AI workloads.

Data Agent Case Study: Elevating AI capabilities : Anthropic[1]

Anthropic, a prominent AI research firm dedicated to developing dependable and interpretable AI systems co-founded by Daniela Amodei, has just incorporated their innovative Claude 3 models into Google Cloud's Vertex AI. This partnership represents a crucial milestone in the advancement of large language models (LLMs) and generative AI, providing enterprises and developers access to Anthropic's state-of-the-art technology within the comprehensive Google Cloud framework.

Anthropic's Claude 3 model family consists of three unique models, carefully engineered to meet various use cases and performance specifications:

- Claude 3 Opus: Anthropic's paramount accomplishment, Opus exhibits near-human proficiency in comprehension and generation across a diverse array of intricate activities.

- Claude 3 Sonnet: The sonnet provides a compelling equilibrium of intellect and efficacy. This approach is designed for large-scale enterprise implementations where rapidity and cost-efficiency are essential.

- Claude 3 Haiku: Haiku is Anthropic's most rapid and concise model, rendering it optimal for applications that emphasize immediate answers and efficient deployment.

The Claude 3 model family is distinguished by the following strengths:

- Improved Reasoning and Problem-Solving: Claude 3 models surpass their predecessors in reasoning capabilities, effectively addressing complicated activities, scientific inquiries, mathematical problems, and coding challenges with increased proficiency.

- Multimodality: These models exhibit advanced visual capabilities. Users can submit photos and obtain textual outputs, facilitating extensive image metadata generation and insights extraction from charts, PDFs, diagrams, and additional formats.

- Multilingual Proficiency: Claude 3 excels in comprehending and producing text in languages other than English.

The accessibility of Claude 3 models on Google Cloud Vertex AI facilitates a range of transformational applications:

- Conversational AI and Chatbots: Create highly interactive and informative chatbots and virtual assistants for customer service, sales assistance, or information retrieval.

- Content Generation and Creative Writing: Expedite the production of diverse writing types, encompassing blog posts, marketing copy, and poetry or fiction.

- Analysis and Insights of Data: Derive essential insights and condense vital information from unstructured data sources, including reports, PDFs, and client feedback.

- Code Generation and Debugging: Optimize the processes of code creation, error resolution, and documentation.

The collaboration between Anthropic and Google Cloud signifies a new epoch in generative AI. Claude 3 in Vertex AI enables businesses and developers to achieve enhanced innovation, efficiency, and customer experience.

SECURITY AGENTS

Security agents enhance security operations by significantly accelerating investigations and automating monitoring and responding to improve vigilance and compliance controls. They can also assist in protecting data and models from cyberattacks, including malicious prompt injection.

Security Agent Case Study: Transformative Unified Workbench for Security Analysts by Exabeam[10]

Exabeam is a worldwide leader in cybersecurity that provides AI-driven security operations. The company was the pioneer in integrating AI and machine learning into its products to provide behavioral analytics in conjunction with security information and event management (SIEM). Currently, the Exabeam Security Operations Platform encompasses cloud-scale security log management and SIEM, robust behavioral analytics, and automated threat detection, investigation, and response (TDIR). Its cloud-native solution suite assists enterprises in identifying risks, mitigating cyberattacks, and overcoming adversaries.

Exabeam analyzes typical behavior and autonomously identifies risky or suspicious activities, enabling security teams to respond more swiftly and effectively, ensuring consistent security results. The firm introduced two innovative cybersecurity capabilities, Threat Center and Exabeam Copilot, to its market-leading AI-driven Exabeam Security Operations Platform. Threat Center is a pioneering integrated platform for threat detection, investigation, and response (TDIR) that streamlines and centralizes the workflows of security analysts, whereas Exabeam Copilot employs generative AI to assist analysts in swiftly comprehending active threats and provides optimal strategies for prompt response. These advanced improvements significantly diminish learning curves for security analysts and enhance their productivity in the SOC.

The business established the Threat Center utilizing Exabeam Copilot to provide security analysts with a streamlined, centralized interface for executing essential TDIR activities, automating mundane tasks, and enhancing investigations for analysts of all proficiency levels. These new features enhance the AI-driven security operations platform, significantly improving analyst productivity, efficiency, and effectiveness. The Threat Center assists security analysts in addressing the issue of excessive fragmented interfaces inside their settings. The integration of Threat Center with Exabeam Copilot enhances the workflows of security analysts. Security operations teams frequently encounter difficulties in handling numerous security products, resulting in fragmented data and insufficient visibility into threats. This complicates the comprehension of their complete danger scenario and hinders the timely execution of TDIR. Exabeam users utilize the Outcomes Navigator function to identify which aspects of their environments may be monitored for TDIR and to determine areas requiring enhanced coverage. The Threat Center optimizes these processes to expedite the remediation of hazards in covered areas. The Exabeam Security Operations Platform utilizes Threat Center and Exabeam Copilot to integrate AI and automation into security operations workflows, providing a comprehensive strategy for addressing cyberthreats, assisting organizations in overcoming automation deficiencies, and expediting response times. The Exabeam platform utilizes AI-driven detection to accurately identify high-risk threats by analyzing the typical behavior of users and entities, prioritizing threats with context-aware risk scoring, all presented through the

Threat Center interface for expedited, precise, and consistent Threat Detection, Investigation, and Response (TDIR).

Threat Center consolidates threat management, investigative tools, and automation to expedite and enhance the investigation and response to threats. Exabeam Copilot enhances security analyst investigations with a sophisticated, security-trained generative AI model. The Threat Center, in conjunction with Exabeam Copilot, assists analysts in comprehending a comprehensive threat that encompasses many detections, hence elucidating the overall narrative of the incident:

- Execute intricate and robust search queries using plain natural language.

- Comprehend a threat and determine an appropriate response by utilizing generative AI threat elucidations for effective inter-organizational communication.

- Automate repetitive jobs, reveal concealed risks, and significantly enhance response times.

- Prioritize warnings and cases utilizing context-sensitive risk assessment.

- Minimize the volume of warnings requiring analyst investigation by implementing detection grouping to associate related entities and events.

- Enhance communication within the SOC team through case sharing, case escalation, and shared documentation.

- Visualize evidence through dynamic threat timelines and immediate access to pertinent data, including behavioral models, users, and endpoints.

- Develop automation protocols essential to Security Operations Center procedures, including the escalation of certain alarms to cases or queues through APIs or webhooks.

- Employ pre-constructed playbooks with options to view, disable, or duplicate for seamless modification.

The AI-driven Exabeam Security Operations Platform not only identifies high-risk threats but also enhances the speed and accuracy of investigations and responses, while enhancing threat coverage, so enabling security teams to maximize their security investments. Additionally announced today, users may now integrate Exabeam TDIR functionalities with their current Microsoft Sentinel deployments. Integrating Exabeam's premier analytics and automation with Microsoft Sentinel enables enterprises to unlock enhanced capabilities from their SIEM. Exabeam enables Microsoft Sentinel users to access new detections with enhanced insights, automate workflows, integrate data from many Microsoft and premier security solutions, and expedite the TDIR functionalities of their SIEM implementation. The

Collector for Microsoft Sentinel expands the increasing array of supported SIEM systems, including Splunk and IBM QRadar, among others.

Security Agent Case Study: Tools to Boost On-Time Payments by Fiserv[44]

Fiserv. Inc. is a United States-based global corporation located in Milwaukee, Wisconsin. Fiserv offers financial technology and services to small and medium-sized company clients within the financial services industry, encompassing banks, thrifts, credit unions, securities broker-dealers, mortgage firms, insurance companies, leasing and finance organizations, and retailers. Small and medium-sized businesses encounter the issue of deferred payments from enterprises, which may subsequently result in financial shortages. Fiserv has introduced a new solution that addresses the challenges SMBs face in collecting funds by expediting the process of accepting ad hoc payments from corporations, which can sometimes result in delays. The organization is now providing billers with additional communication options to expedite payment processing. The new functionalities enable billers to integrate call-to-action notifications and alerts into current workflows, facilitating the dispatch of individualized bill payment reminders or messages via email, SMS, phone calls, or interactive voice response systems. Call-to-action notifications and alerts augment the established billing and payment functionalities with straightforward, contemporary, and economical communications that seamlessly interact with clients' ERP systems.

These notifications are facilitated by a connection with Fiserv's BillMatrix service, enabling billers to offer "choice and convenience while decreasing costs and minimizing operational complexities. "The system also incorporates the communication platform Tilli, which is a cloud-based customer communication platform as a service and a global payment stack. This new product is introduced at a time when timely payments have become increasingly crucial for small to medium-sized enterprises (SMBs). This is due to the fact that 80% of small and medium-sized businesses receive compensation through ad hoc payments for the items and services they offer to larger corporations. For small and medium-sized businesses, ad hoc transactions constitute merely a little fraction of the payments made to their vendors and customers. However, for the majority of small and medium-sized businesses, these sporadic, non-recurring payments have become integral to their standard revenue stream. Ad hoc payments currently constitute roughly seventy-five percent of the accounts receivable (AR) volume in dollars for small and medium-sized businesses (SMBs). However, small and medium-sized businesses (SMBs) receive ad hoc payments for various reasons, with 81% receiving such payments in exchange for both products and services in a typical year. Fiserv discovered that with the introduction of the new offering, the percentage of small and medium-sized businesses (SMBs) receiving ad hoc payments for products or services has risen, establishing it as a favored option for SMB clients.

Security Agent Case Study: Security Innovation in Financial Services: BBVA[20]

BBVA partnered with Google Cloud to build innovative artificial intelligence (AI) and machine learning (ML) models aimed at predicting and preventing cyberattacks on its banking infrastructure, thereby enhancing security for the bank and its clients. BBVA is the inaugural bank in Europe to implement Chronicle, Google Cloud's security analytics platform that enables teams to consolidate and analyze all their security data in a single location for the detection and investigation of threats at scale.

BBVA has collaborated with Google to create a new platform that enables the bank to implement more modern technology in a cost-efficient and scalable environment. The integration of Google Cloud's Chronicle with BBVA's security operations expertise will empower the bank to utilize superior AI capabilities for cyberattack prevention. This collaboration has advanced the bank, positioning it in the front of safeguarding its financial infrastructure and clientele against security risks.

CREATIVE AGENTS

Creative agents may enhance your company by providing superior design and production expertise, collaborating on images, presentations, and conceptual development with employees. Numerous firms are developing agents for their marketing teams, audio and video production teams, and all creative individuals in need of assistance. Creative agents enable individuals to assume the roles of designer, artist, or producer.

Creative Agent Case Study: Grupo Globo 's Transformation as a Mediatech Company[4]

Grupo Globo is a Brazilian private entertainment and mass media corporation headquartered in Rio de Janeiro, Brazil. Established in 1925 by Irineu Marinho, it is the preeminent media group in Latin America and ranks among the greatest media corporations globally. Grupo Globo's assets encompass over-the-air broadcasting, television and film production, pay television subscription services, streaming media, publishing, and online services. The principal assets comprise the flagship television network TV Globo; the pay television content division Canais Globo, which includes cable networks such as GloboNews, GNT, Multishow, SporTV, Viva, Gloob, and the premium film network Telecine; the film production entity Globo Filmes; the radio operator Sistema Globo de Rádio; the publishing houses Editora Globo and Infoglobo; and the streaming service Globoplay.

Brazilian media conglomerate Globo has established a long-term strategic alliance with Google Cloud in its endeavor to transform into a comprehensive mediatech enterprise. The new agreement seeks to enhance scalability, efficiency, and innovation within Globo's operations and distribution. This strategic alliance aims to expedite the primary pillars of our change, including public focus, data management, innovative partnerships, and new business models. It will leverage Google's expertise in data management, artificial intelligence (AI), and machine learning (ML), along with its global, scalable, and secure infrastructure, to enhance the company's digital transformation.

The company is confronting the challenge of managing substantial content consumption from programs like 'Big Brother Brazil, ' resulting in Globo's platforms achieving some of their highest audience ratings in decades and reaching historic milestones on the streaming service "Globoplay, " including a record of three million votes per minute in the 21st season. Globo has exceeded 100 million monthly active users (MAU) and 100 million Globo IDs within its identity management system, enabling it to leverage the scale and AI/ML (artificial intelligence/machine learning) capabilities of Google Cloud to provide a distinctive and personalized experience for its users.

Through this partnership, the business intends to merge internet and broadcast to facilitate a more seamless and complimentary navigation between digital and linear platforms. It also seeks to investigate novel opportunities for hyper-segmentation of the content offering, tailoring suggestions in real time for its audience.

The native integration of Globoplay into the Android TV OS presents new options for the company to provide consumers a seamless and distinctive experience of accessing free-to-air digital TV and enjoying on-demand programming via Globoplay.

Creative Agent Case Study: Canva ups utilization by AI-driven Magic Studio[39]

Canva is a visual communication platform utilized by over 175 million individuals monthly for creating presentations, movies, papers, websites, social media graphics, and additional content. A significant proportion of global knowledge workers lack design expertise; yet, Canva's user-friendly interface, extensive libraries, and efficient tools enable anyone to produce visually engaging material.

Canva asserts that AI has the potential to revolutionize and expedite the creative process, enhancing design accessibility and efficiency for individuals of all skill levels. Canva utilized OpenAI as the basic technology to rapidly equip customers with various capabilities inside its AI suite, Magic Studio. Canva intended

Magic Studio to serve as a cohesive creative suite that integrates the finest AI technology into one platform. Although Canva has utilized AI in its offerings for years, the incorporation of generative AI tools posed a nuanced problem, necessitating the enhancement of functionalities without disrupting the user experience. Ultimately, Canva's reputation is founded on its ability to offer an accessible method for creating high-quality material, even for amateur designers.

Magic Studio needed to guarantee the seamless integration of diverse modalities—text, image, video—without inundating the user. OpenAI's GPT-4 proficiently integrated multimodalities into a cohesive workflow, enabling Canva to provide sophisticated AI product features while preserving an intuitive user experience. For Canva, delivering robust and secure AI technology was essential to advancing the realm of design. Canva utilized the creative capabilities of GPT-4 to enhance many features within Magic Studio. The company offered the following features in Magic Studio:

- Magic Write: A writing tool utilizing OpenAI's API. Magic Write not only generates text in response to prompts but is also optimized to assist with every phase of the writing process, including planning, paragraph generation, rewriting, paraphrasing, grammatical checking, and summarization. Users in various languages and content formats have composed over 10 billion words utilizing Magic Write.

- Magic Design: Canva's design creation tool integrates OpenAI's API with Canva's own AI design engine and a repository of over 100 million elements and templates.

Users can make presentations, social media postings, and videos by entering a prompt for their desired creation.

- Magic Switch : This function transforms a single design into numerous alternative formats with the press of a button. Canva utilizes OpenAI's API and visual technologies to analyze and comprehend content designs, ranging from whiteboards to presentations. Magic Switch may summarize, translate, reorganize, or convert content into another format, such as an email or song lyrics. The user simply needs to specify their request, such as "convert this poster to a presentation in French" or "alter this document to a horizontal orientation. " OpenAI's GPT-4 model facilitates immediate translation in over 100 languages.

The internal AI development team at Canva recognized the potential for accelerated progress through direct collaboration with OpenAI. They wanted to develop AI solutions that comply with client trust and safety guidelines while fostering innovation. OpenAI's comprehensive safety protocols and measures, enhanced by cooperation with the Trust and Safety teams of each platform, instill confidence in Canva to implement safe and responsible AI.

Canva's close collaboration with OpenAI encompasses more than just Magic Studio. The native DALL-E application facilitates the effortless creation of high-quality photographs from within Canva. This custom GPT has demonstrated significant efficacy in acquiring new users for Canva. As of now, individuals globally have utilized Canva's AI products over 5 billion times.

Creative Agent Case Study:Transforming Product Campaign Development at PUMA[22]

PUMA is a premier global sports brand that specializes in the design, development, sale, and marketing of footwear, apparel, and accessories. For over 75 years, PUMA has consistently advanced sport and culture by developing rapid items for the world's swiftest players. PUMA provides performance and sport-oriented lifestyle items across areas like Football, Running and Training, Basketball, Golf, and Motorsports. It partners with esteemed designers and businesses to integrate sports elements into street culture and fashion. The PUMA Group possesses the brands PUMA, Cobra Golf, and stichd. The company distributes its products throughout over 120 countries, employs around 20,000 individuals globally, and is based in Germany.

The firm collaborated with Google to improve the internet buying experience for millions of PUMA customers globally with generative AI. PUMA was the inaugural company in its sector to implement AI-generated imagery extensively in its online store. By utilizing Imagen 2 on Vertex AI, PUMA can now generate dynamic and tailored product photography, enhancing click-through rates and expediting the time-to-market for PUMA's worldwide digital campaigns.

Employing Imagen 2 on Vertex AI, PUMA may produce pertinent visuals, including customized background images specific to the product, consumer, and area. Although the technology is internationally accessible, Imagen on Vertex AI enables marketers in distinct PUMA regions to customize content according to their own market requirements. For instance, when online buying, consumers in Japan can encounter a lifestyle shoe featured on the streets of Ginza or a trail running shoe showcased in the foothills of Mt. Fuji. In addition to image synthesis, Imagen on Vertex AI serves as a robust instrument for image editing, assisting PUMA content editors with labor-intensive tasks, like shadowing, composition, color accuracy, resolution, and product positioning.

PUMA's retail teams have enhanced average order value (AOV) through improved personalized content utilizing Google Cloud's data and AI tools, while also significantly decreasing the time required to launch products, allowing for immediate product availability upon arrival at the warehouse.

PUMA will soon examine Imagen 3, Google Cloud's most recent and superior text-to-image model, as it progresses and expands campaign development in the future. The sports company intends to broaden the deployment of Google Cloud's Vertex AI Search for Retail to further subsidiaries to enhance average order value and total shopper conversion rate.

Creative Agent Case Study: Writing Differentiated Product Descriptions in One Hour at Adore Me[54]

Adore Me is a US-based direct-to-consumer intimate apparel brand established in 2011. They were the inaugural intimate clothing manufacturer to provide extended sizing to the market in 2013. As a certified B corporation, sustainability is integral to all aspects of its operations. Furthermore, they concentrate on technology, innovation, and exploring novel methods to support our clientele.

Since attaining certification as a B Corporation, adherence to sustainability has increasingly influenced their content production methods. They needed collaboration with a partner capable of developing style guides for company-wide implementation. They collaborated with Writer. Writer is a comprehensive generative AI platform designed for organizations. It assists enterprises in developing highly tailored AI applications that streamline entire business processes, accommodate intricate use cases, and integrate organizational intelligence into workflows.

The company began prioritizing use cases by developing a two-by-two matrix. One axis indicated the degree of structure in the text, with elements such as an email subject line or a product description being highly structured, whereas entirely original online copy for a marketing campaign is considered unstructured. On the other axis, they indicated the revenue risk, specifically its degree of elevation or reduction. The writer assisted Adore Me in addressing content opportunities that are well-organized yet pose a minimal income risk. The organization deemed it essential to include the perspective of a risk manager into the creation of every content. The optimal starting points were determined as content components that would not incur significant negative consequences if they are not flawless.

The initial application was product descriptions. It demonstrated significant success due to its efficiency and simplicity, aligning with Adore Me's overarching company philosophy. During the summer of 2022, iOS 14 interrupted internet acquisition, rendering SEO a priority. Adore Me developed an AI application utilizing Writer to produce product-recommended descriptions that were extensively optimized for SEO.

Adore Me offers products only in sets, although the phrase "bra and panty set" may not be the most intuitive; still, it accurately reflects consumer search behavior. The Writer app significantly augmented the search volume for that particular term by training the model to respond to that precise inquiry. The organization had a 40% rise in non-branded search.

Adore Me utilized Writer AI services for a program named Dailylook, which is a home try-on service. The consumer receives a package containing four to eight items, from which they may select the ones they wish to retain and return the remainder. A human stylist aids consumers in selecting things and includes a handwritten note. Adore Me experienced a notable increase in the quantity of things retained by customers when a message was dispatched, stating, "I believe you will appreciate this product for this reason, this product complements another product effectively, and this is how you can style them in conjunction. "

In these notes, the stylists composed 400 to 500 words more than one thousand times daily. The process was monotonous and arduous, exemplifying how managers at Adore Me utilized the AI application to generate an initial draft with appropriate language and style. The stylist remained informed, however there were preliminary concerns regarding the reception of this process adjustment. The stylists expressed great satisfaction with the initial versions of the notes created by the writer.

Utilizing Writer AI for note writing enabled the organization to observe a significant increase in stylist productivity, as the time required for note composition was reduced by 36%. Adore Me further utilized the AI Studio of Writer for application development. Upon entering the Mexican market with Adore Me Mexico, the company faced a significant challenge with translation. The company utilized AI Studio, engaging a small team comprising a prompt organizer, a merchandiser, and a native Mexican Spanish speaker to operate within the no-code platform. They commenced with the English input, attempting a direct translation into Spanish, but subsequently recognized the potential to enhance the translation by incorporating an additional layer.

They incorporated an additional prompt to solicit comments for enhancing the generated translation for a consumer in Mexico seeking stylish products from an intimate apparel brand. This enabled the Adore Me marketers to delve into the subtleties of selling to consumers in Mexican Spanish. It is not merely a translation. This is being accomplished without a developer. Utilizing the Writer Framework, they transformed this into a continuous application in which the end user remains unaware of the prompt. The team could simultaneously process 2,900 product descriptions, obtain the output in a CSV format, and subsequently post them to the Adore Me Mexico website via their proprietary backend. Another endeavor including AI Studio was Adore Me's expansion into additional marketplaces, affectionately termed 'Adore Me Everywhere' by the team. The objective was to facilitate the acquisition of Adore Me products on macy. com, target. com, Walmart, Amazon, and victoriasecret. com and the parent corporation. Each of these markets has distinct regulations and prerequisites for their product descriptions. Prior to Writer, a member of the merchandising team was required to manually edit product descriptions for each channel. This constituted a significant constraint on market entry velocity.

The prompt coordinator and merchandiser collaborated on the no-code aspect of AI Studio, enabling users to input a product ID into the application, which would then automatically generate product descriptions for each channel. Additionally, one can publish straight to the Adore Me website via the Writer Framework application.

The third-party marketplace descriptions application has enabled the organization to reduce a 20-hour monthly process to merely 20 minutes. The time savings were significant due to the previously cumbersome manual approach. The application conserved time and liberated staff to engage in more valuable tasks.

Creative Agent Case Study: Radisson Hotel Group Personalize Event Experiences with AI[29]

Radisson Hotel Group is a global hotel conglomerate, functioning in the EMEA and APAC regions, with more than 1,320 hotels now operational and under development throughout over

95 countries. The worldwide hotel group is swiftly developing a strategy to substantially increase its portfolio. The Group's primary brand commitment is "Every Moment Matters," accompanied by a distinctive "Yes I Can!" service philosophy. The portfolio of the Radisson family of brands encompasses Radisson Collection, art'otel, Radisson Blu, Radisson, Radisson RED, Radisson Individuals, Park Plaza, Park Inn by Radisson, Country Inn & Suites by Radisson, and prizeotel, all unified under the commercial umbrella of Radisson Hotels. Radisson Rewards is the loyalty program of Radisson Hotel Group, designed to provide an enhanced experience that emphasizes the significance of every moment. The program, recognized for its efficiency, offers members outstanding perks that are accessible immediately at several hotels in Europe, the Middle East, Africa, and the Asia Pacific region. Radisson Meetings offers customized solutions for various events or meetings, including hybrid options that prioritize guests and their requirements.

Radisson Meetings is founded on three robust service commitments: Personal, Professional, and Memorable, while adhering to fundamental excellence and maintaining a distinctive 100% Carbon Neutral status. The chain has lately introduced two new technology-driven products. Radisson Meetings Unbound is a platform centered on immersive information and digital replicas, transforming how conference planners examine meeting spaces and various configurations. The new AI-driven application will enable users to book directly or submit a request for a proposal for that particular space, accompanied by immersive virtual tours featuring floor plans, dollhouse views, and precise digital reproductions of the hotel. This technology encompasses in-house event teams, enabling them to display various meeting room configurations in real-time via any smartphone or VR goggles. The group simultaneously unveiled its additional AI-driven Radisson Meetings Dream Machine product.

This solution employs a tailored Generative AI tool to assist event professionals from conceptualization to visualization. They can now utilize the platform to generate graphic depictions of their desired event settings.

Event inspiration is disseminated through thought leadership blogs, including one on the group's site titled "How to Personalize Event Experiences with AI, " as well as through genuine case studies of successful event designs. The Group introduced the new technology-driven products by conducting a series of interactive creative workshops and "infinity rooms" in prominent locations throughout Europe and Africa. The "infinity room" by Radisson Hotel Group offers an immersive experience aimed at encouraging event planners to transcend their comfort zones and innovate their strategies for meetings and events. Upon entering an almost dark conference room, participants engage in a sequence of deep-focus visualization exercises designed to reflect on the issues encountered in organizing meetings and to plan solutions for various event limitations.

As organizers advance through the various phases of event preparation, the space progressively brightens, gradually unveiling infinite patterns intended to promote co-creation and collaborative invention. The inaugural "infinity room" was recently unveiled at Park Inn by Radisson Amsterdam City West. The Radisson Meetings Dream Machine events tour will proceed with innovative and engaging events in Düsseldorf, Copenhagen, Manchester, and Johannesburg in the next months[40].

Bibliography

1. Adam Blackington (2024, March 11). Anthropic's Claude 3 Models: Elevating AI Capabilities On Google Cloud Vertex AI. *Adam Blackington. blog.* https://adamblackington. blog/ anthropics-claude-3-models-elevating-ai-capabilities-on-google-cloud-vertex-ai/

2. Aimee Meester (2024, May, 31). Marketing 2. 0: Embracing The AI-Powered Future. *Forbes.* https://www. forbes. com/ councils/forbesbusinesscouncil/2024/05/31/marketing-20-embracing-the-ai-powered-future

3. Amanda Sellers (2016, June, 14). What is the buyer's journey? *Hubspot.* https://blog. hubspot. com/sales/what-is-the-buyers-journey?

4. Anna Marie de la Fuente (2021, April, 07). Brazil's Globo Pacts with Google Cloud in Bid to Become a Mediatech Company. *Variety.* https://variety. com/2021/digital/global/ globo-google-cloud-mediatech-company-1234945642/

5. AWS Startups (2025, February 04). Mendel reimagines how healthcare workers interface with patient data on AWS. https://aws. amazon. com/startups/learn/mendel-reimagines-how-healthcare-workers-interface-with-patient-data-on-aws

6. Bayer (2024 November, 14). *Bayer's recent FieldView release turns farm information into answers.* https://www. bayer. com/en/us/news-stories/fieldview-features

7. Bloomberg (2023, May, 05). *AI levels playing field for startups, Big Tech in Asia.* https://economictimes. indiatimes. com/ tech/technology/ai-levels-playing-field-for-startups-big-tech-in-asia

8. Boston Consulting Group (2022, July 7). *Online retail spending to reach US$ 300 billion by 2030: Report.* https:// indbiz. gov. in/online-retail-spending-to-reach-us-300-billion-by-2030-report

9. Brianna LaRouche (2024, March, 27) RS Implements GroupBy's eCommerce Search and Product Discovery Platform powered by Google Cloud Vertex AI Search for Retail. *Businesswire.* https://www. businesswire. com/news/ home/20240327667520/en/RS-Implements-GroupBys-eCommerce-Search-and-Product-Discovery-Platform-powered-by-Google-Cloud-Vertex-AI-Search-for-Retail

10. Businesswire (2024, February, 27). *Exabeam Introduces Transformative Unified Workbench for Security Analysts with Generative AI Assistance.* https://www. businesswire. com/ news/home/20240227404817/en/Exabeam-Introduces-Transformative-Unified-Workbench-for-Security-Analysts-with-Generative-AI-Assistance

11. Calls9 (2025, February 20). *Generative AI-Powered Creativity: Insights from major brands for your business.* https://www. calls9. com/blogs/generative-ai-powered-creativity-insights-from-major-brands-for-your-business.

12. Carmel McCarthy (2023, December, 12). Hiscox and Google Cloud Collaborate on AI in lead underwriting for the London Market. *Hiscoxgroup.* https://www. hiscoxgroup. com/news/press-releases/2023/12-12-23

13. David Mosyan (2024, Oct 05). How companies use AI (GCP). *Medium.* https://medium. com/@dmosyan/how-companies-use-ai-gcp-6d2fb59e7cde

14. Elissa Hudson (2021, July, 07). How to blend web analytics and digital marketing analytics to grow better? *Hubspot.* https://blog. hubspot. com/marketing/digital-marketing-analytics?

15. Eric Fershtman (2024, August, 13). CareerVillage Launches Coach, First-of-its-Kind AI Career Development Tool Built for Equity and Measurable Results. *Prnewswire.* https:// www. prnewswire. com/news-releases/careervillage-launches-coach-first-of-its-kind-ai-career-development-tool-built-for-equity-and-measurable-results-302219163. html

16. Explore Business Bell. ca (2024, April 9): *Bell Canada and Google Cloud power an AI-driven contact centre revolution.* https://explore. business. bell. ca/news-and-events/bell-canada-partners-google-cloud-power-ai-driven-contact-centre-revolution-canadian-businesses

17. Google (2023, May, 19). *Best Practices Guide: AI Essentials in Google Ads.* https://ads. google. com/intl/en_in/home/resources/articles/ai-essentials/

18. Google (2024, March, 01). *The AI handbook: Resources and tools to help marketers get started.* https://www. thinkwithgoogle. com/intl/en-emea/marketing-strategies/automation/ai-handbook/

19. Google (2024, September, 24). *185 real-world gen AI use cases from the world's leading organizations.* https://cloud. google. com/transform/101-real-world-generative-ai-use-cases-from-industry-leaders

20. Google Cloud (2021, February 23). *BBVA and Google Cloud Form Strategic Partnership to Drive Security Innovation in Financial Services.* https://www. prnewswire. com/ news-releases/bbva-and-google-cloud-form-strategic-partnership-to-drive-security-innovation-in-financial-services-301232385. html

21. Google Cloud (2024, September, 24). *ScottsMiracle-Gro and Google Cloud Announce New Collaboration to Transform Consumer Experiences Using Generative AI.* https://www. googlecloudpresscorner. com/2024-09-24-ScottsMiracle-Gro-and-GoogleCloud Announce-New-Collaboration-to-Transform-Consumer-Experiences-Using-Generative-AI

22. Google Cloud (2024, September, 24). *PUMA Transforms Product Campaign Development with Google Cloud's Generative AI.* https://www. prnewswire. com/news-releases/ puma-transforms-product-campaign-development-with-google-clouds-generative-ai-302256616. html

23. Google Cloud (2023, May 10). *Character. AI and Google Cloud Partner to Build the Next Generation of Conversational AI.* https://www. prnewswire. com/news-releases/characterai-and-google-cloud-partner-to-build-the-next-generation-of-conversational-ai-301821277. html

24. GoTo (2024, July, 16). *GoTo launches new AI strategy with the introduction of Dira, the first ever AI based fintech Voice Assistant in Bahasa Indonesia.* https://www. gotocompany.

com/en/news/press/goto-launches-new-ai-strategy-with-the-introduction-of-dira-the-first-ever-ai-based-fintech-voice-assistant-in-bahasa-indonesia

25. Hootsuite (2024, Feb 29). *How a Kidney Care Company Drove 42% More Job Applications from LinkedIn.* https://www. hootsuite. com/resources/davita?srsltid=AfmBOopiCYTQFrOinh0V_td_ZA7hQ53KVGPonalovFJzairJeXx6sNtu

26. Investor. dnb (2024, August, 02). *Dun & Bradstreet Introduces Gen AI Capabilities to D&B Hoovers™ Sales Intelligence Solution.* https://investor. dnb. com/news/news-details/2024/Dun--Bradstreet-Introduces-Gen-AI-Capabilities-to-DB-Hoovers-Sales-Intelligence-Solution/default. aspx

27. Investor. gm(2023, August, 28). *General Motors Teams Up with Google Cloud on AI Initiatives.* https://investor. gm. com/news-releases/news-release-details/general-motors-teams-google-cloud-ai-initiatives

28. Karen Walke (2022, September 14). Lessons From Formula E Racing For High-Performance Teams. *Forbes.* https://www. forbes. com/sites/karenwalker/2022/09/14/lessons-from-formula-e-racing-for-high-performance-teams/

29. Kate Harden-England (2024, March 18). Radisson hotel group launches AI-powered meeting and event product. *Travolution.* https://www. travolution. com/news/technology/radisson-hotel-group-launches-ai-powered-meeting-and-event-product/

30. Labelbox (2024, May, 01). *Google Cloud powers LLM evaluation service with Labelbox.* https://labelbox. com/customers/google-cloud-llm-evaluation/

31. Manish Gupta (2022, December, 19). Google for India 2022: Driving impact with AI across Indian languages, the agricultural ecosystem, and digitizing your doctor's penmanship. *Google.* https://blog. google/intl/en-in/company-news/inside-google/google-for-india-2022-ai-announcements/

32. Martin Coulter (2024, May 15). Data crunching keeps England ahead of the game, AI to unearth new gems. *Reuters.* https://www. reuters. com/sports/soccer/data-crunching-keeps-england-ahead-game-ai-unearth-new-gems-2024-05-15/

33. Mike Lieberman (2024, May, 5). 7. 5 tips and tricks to improve marketing campaign performance by 10x. *Square2Marketing.* https://www. square2marketing. com/blog/7. 5-tips-and-tricks-to-improve-marketing-campaign-performance-by-10x

34. Monostori, L. (2014). Artificial Intelligence. In: Laperrière, L. , Reinhart, G. (eds) CIRP Encyclopedia of Production Engineering. Springer, Berlin, Heidelberg. https://doi. org/10. 1007/978-3-642-20617-7_16703

35. Nasscom Community (2022, June, 23). *NASSCOM AI Gamechangers 2022 Compendium.* https://community. nasscom. in/communities/ai/ai-gamechangers-2022-realizing-indias-ai-promise

36. Nasscom (2022). *Nasscom Tech Start-Up Report 2022 – Rising Above Uncertainty: The 2022 Saga Of Indian Tech Start-Ups.* https://nasscom. in/knowledge-center/publications/nasscom-tech-start-report-2022-rising-above-uncertainty-2022

37. Nidhi Bhardwaj (2022, December, 31). How AI-enabled initiatives have impacted these Indian sectors in 2022. *Indiatoday.* https://www. indiatoday. in/cryptocurrency/story/how-ai-enabled-initiatives-have-impacted-these-indian-sectors-in-2022-2315839-2022-12-31

38. Nuria Cordón (2024, April, 09). How Ipsos has digitally adapted to changing business needs. *CIO.* https://www. cio. com/article/2083838/how-ipsos-has-digitally-adapted-to-changing-business-needs. html

39. Open AI (2024, May 16). *Canva's AI-powered Magic Studio used 5 billion times and counting.* https://openai. com/index/canva/

40. Radisson Hotels (2024, March, 14). *Radisson Hotel Group launches visionary Radisson Meetings Unbound and AI-powered Radisson Meetings Dream Machine.* https://www. radissonhotels. com/en-us/corporate/media/press-releases/RHG-launches-Radisson-Meetings-Unbound-and-Radisson-Meetings-Dream-Machine

41. Sabrina Sanchez (2024, June 20). How Tombras used Google's Gemini to create over 6, 000 hyperlocal ads for PODS. *AdAge.* https://adage. com/article/special-report-cannes-lions/how-tombras-used-ai-create-6000-location-based-ads-pods/2566186

42. Simon Kemp (2024, January, 31). The time we spend on social media. *Datareportal.* https://datareportal. com/reports/digital-2024-deep-dive-the-time-we-spend-on-social-media

43. Press Information Bureau, Govt. of India (2024). *Economic Survey of India 2023-24.* https://static. pib. gov.

in/WriteReadData/specificdocs/documents/2024/jul/
doc2024722351601. pdf

44. Pymnts (2024, April, 30). *Fiserv Debuts Communication Tools to Boost On-Time Payments.* https://www. pymnts. com/news/b2b-payments/2024/fiserv-debuts-communication-tools-to-boost-on-time-payments/

45. Quantum Metric (2024, April 04). *Quantum Metric simplifies digital customer listening with Gen AI powered solution.* https://www. prnewswire. com/news-releases/quantum-metric-simplifies-digital-customer-listening-with-gen-ai-powered-solution-302107814. html

46. Rajiv Gupta, Sumit Sarawgi, Vikash Jain, Sudhanshu Chawla, Harsh Singh, Sangeeta Gupta, Achyuta Ghosh, Namita Jain. (2022, December, 07). Sandboxing Into The Future – Decoding Technology's Biggest Bets. *Boston Consulting Group. https://www. bcg. com/publications/2022/india-sandboxing-into-the-future-decoding-technologys-biggest-bets*

47. Robert Silk (2024, May 02) Alaska Airlines using generative AI flight searches. *Travel Weekly.* https://www. travelweekly. com/Travel-News/Airline-News/Alaska-Airlines-using-generative-AI-flight-searches

48. Snap (2024, Sept 24). *Snap Partners with Google Cloud to Power Multi-Modal Generative AI Experiences Within My AI.* https://newsroom. snap. com/snap-google-gemini-my-ai

49. Stewart Townsend. (2024, April, 8). The Future of AI in Marketing: Predictions for 2024. *Medium.* https://medium. com/@channelasaservice/the-future-of-ai-in-marketing-predictions-for-2024

50. Sunny Bets (2024, February, 06). 7 Types of Artificial Intelligence, From chatbots to super-robots, here's the types of AI to know and where the tech's headed. *Builtin.* nexthttps://builtin. com/artificial-intelligence/types-of-artificial-intelligence

51. Tech Wire (March 08, 2024). *AI in Construction and Engineering: Building the Future.* https://gamuda. com. my/2024/03/ai-in-construction-and-engineering-building-the-future/news/

52. Vangelis Moraitis (2024, Oct, 06). AI in Business: Real-World Use Cases and Success Stories. *the AI track.* https:// theaitrack. com/ai-in-business-use-cases/

53. Viswanath Pilla (2023, March, 01). Healthtech startup SigTuple raises Rs 34. 5 crore in funding from Endiya Partners, Accel. *Economictimes.* https://economictimes. indiatimes. com/tech/funding/healthtech-startup-sigtuple-raises-rs-34-5-crore-from-endiya-partners-accel/articleshow/98332657. cms?from=mdr

54. Writer's room (2024, July, 02). *Retail reimagined: Adore Me accelerates time to market with Writer AI Studio.* https:// writer. com/blog/adore-me-customer-story/

www.ingramcontent.com/pod-product-compliance
Lightning Source LLC
Chambersburg PA
CBHW021356150726
47989CB00005B/2273